1971

SONG.

# POETRY AND SONG
## IN THE
## GERMAN BAROQUE

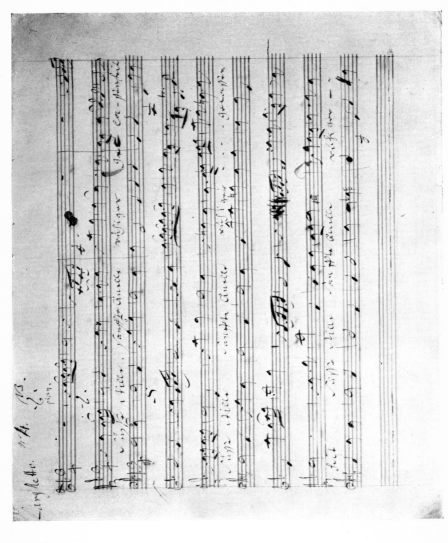

From the manuscript (in the British Museum) of Handel's setting of Brockes's poem
*Süße Stille, sanfte Quelle*

R. HINTON THOMAS

⤙⤙⤙ ❀ ⤚⤚⤚

# POETRY AND SONG
# IN THE
# GERMAN BAROQUE

⤙⤙⤙ ❀ ⤚⤚⤚

*A Study of the Continuo Lied*

OXFORD

*At the Clarendon Press*

1963

*Oxford University Press, Amen House, London E.C.4*

GLASGOW  NEW YORK  TORONTO  MELBOURNE  WELLINGTON
BOMBAY  CALCUTTA  MADRAS  KARACHI  LAHORE  DACCA
CAPE TOWN  SALISBURY  NAIROBI  IBADAN  ACCRA
KUALA LUMPUR  HONG KONG

PRINTED IN GREAT BRITAIN

# PREFACE

As anyone at all familiar with German baroque music will appreciate, a comprehensive account of the continuo lied would involve a veritable array of minor figures, most of whom would add nothing essential to the total picture. I have preferred a more economical and selective method, using analyses of carefully selected songs as focal points of larger and more general issues, and arranging them in accordance with a significant line of development. Also, this book is not a history of the continuo lied, but an inquiry into the relationship, in the lied, of poetry and music, and this has necessarily influenced my selection. It has led me to disregard a number of composers who could not be passed over in a book governed only by musical considerations, and, as far as possible, I have chosen my songs so that the text of each has some merit or interest as poetry.

It is because this book is concerned with the continuo lied that Schütz and J. S. Bach figure only incidentally, and, in view of the predominant direction of the German continuo lied in this period, I have placed my emphasis on secular song. The poems dealt with in Chapter X are religious, but Briegel's song-cycle claims attention for various reasons. It occurs at a critical juncture in the history of the baroque lied and is not otherwise available in a complete modern edition. Moreover, Gryphius, though the best of the German baroque poets, was conspicuously neglected by other composers, and my subject required that a place should be found for him in my book.

Musical quotations are transcribed into their modern form, but, as in the original practice, only the bass line is given in the continuo part. A simple realization of the bass, especially in the longer examples, could give an inadequate, and even misleading, impression to those unfamiliar with the proper performance of baroque music, and experts will be in a position to fill out the bass with their own improvisations. The only exception to this principle occurs in Chapter XII, where my analysis of a song of Handel requires detailed reference to the fuller harmonic implications. Musical and literary titles are given as in the original, but, as far as possible, texts of songs and quotations from poetry have been modernized to ease matters for readers who may be musicians rather than German scholars.

I must express my gratitude to publishers who most generously have allowed me to reprint musical material. Messrs. Breitkopf & Härtel gave me permission to use a considerable number of musical examples without which my book would have been much the poorer, and, where I wanted to do so, allowed me to quote pieces in their complete form. Copyright still applies to a number of these, and I am asked particularly to refer to the examples taken from Schering's *Geschichte der Musik in Beispielen* and from Roth's revised edition of Handel's *Neun Deutsche Arien*. I am most grateful for these concessions, and likewise to the Möseler Verlag, who kindly acceded to my request to reprint two pieces of Senfl. The firm of Heinrich Buschmann, successor to the rights of the former Helios Verlag, likewise let me use two songs from *Das frühdeutsche Lied* by Professor W. Vetter, to whose pioneering work all students of German baroque song are indebted, and who was so good as to waive his author's rights in the matter. In all these instances the music appears for all practical purposes as in the source, except that in some instances additional bar lines have been added, and, as already mentioned, the realization of the continuo has been omitted. In the case of Handel's setting of *Süße Stille, sanfte Quelle* the figuring of the bass has been slightly added to after comparison of Roth's version with Handel's manuscript in the British Museum.

I owe much to Professor Roy Pascal for advice on many points concerning the literary aspects, and to Dr. Nigel Fortune, who likewise was so kind as to read my manuscript and from whose expert knowledge of baroque music I have been allowed to benefit in many different ways. I must not fail to mention the stimulus of many discussions with Professor Wilfrid Mellers, now of Pittsburgh University, through whom, I fancy, I first became aware of the possibilities and importance of such a subject. I am grateful to John Coates for help on various technical questions, and to Anthony Ford for his skill and patience in the task of transcription.

R. H. T.

*October 1962*

# CONTENTS

PART III

# INTRODUCTION

## The Two Voices of the Baroque

WHEN J. S. Bach was born in 1685, the creative period of baroque lyrical poetry was virtually finished, and the last significant writers died in that decade. At Bach's death in 1750 German poetry was set on quite a different course. Hagedorn's *Oden und Lieder* had begun to appear ten years before, and, in the songs of Telemann and Görner, at once began to play a crucial part in the transition of the lied to its post-baroque situation.

Composers now wanted their songs to be simple, natural, and easy to perform. Compared with much baroque music, the baroque lied could have been so described, but, by the time Telemann published his *24 Oden* and Görner his *Sammlung Neuer Oden und Lieder*, this was more or less forgotten, and the outspoken hostility of poets and composers to the baroque was directed above all against aspects that were least conspicuous in the lied. Scheibe illustrates this in his well-known criticism of Bach, who came to epitomize the essentially baroque to many to whom Adam Krieger was little more than a name. Another factor, contrasting with the trend of interest in poetry and music towards reason, nature, and 'good taste', was baroque architecture, which developed late in relation to poetry and music. The creation in the period from about 1720 to 1750 of many of the most famous and lavish buildings, ecclesiastical and secular, greatly encouraged the identification of baroque with what in the circumstances was likely to appear as merely extravagant disorder. Largely through architecture baroque came to imply above all (and in the popular image has remained predominantly associated with) ornamental profusion and pretentious extravagance, 'all that . . . suggests splendour and wealth by sheer abundance and lavishness of colour'.[1] In church after church now being converted into the baroque style these were the characteristics that caught the eye, and the same applies to the *Residenzen*, the princely courts, whose ambitions of grandeur and self-glorification were the driving force behind the cult of opera.

It is true to say of a good deal of baroque music, with its continuity of rhythm and consistency of figuration, its 'strikingly "parallel"

[1] Richard Hoggart, *The Uses of Literacy*, Pelican edition, Harmondsworth, 1958, p. 114.

arrangement of the structure . . . the habit of continuing for a long time in a uniform manner . . . preference for "objective" movement, for an almost mathematical regularity', that it is 'cosmic rather than human',[1] and it is tempting even to relate these features to a concept of exalted power, sublimely poised above the foibles and contingencies of ordinary mortals. The lied, however, is representative of its time in a different way, and it contrasts with these and some other character-istic manifestations of the baroque, like the figural music, for example, of the kind indicated by Christoph Bernard, Schütz's pupil, when he said that 'in our time music has reached such heights that, in view of the great number of figures . . . it can be likened to rhetoric'.[2] Such music, typified by the application to music of figures familiar in rhetoric and to some extent borrowed from it, and sometimes coloured by Luther's idea of music as *praedicatio sonora*, came often from the cantors, and the gap between this kind of music and the lied is reflected, in the history of the lied, in the small part played by the cantors, including Bach. He has hardly any place at all,[3] though also he came on the scene when the lied had largely ceased to attract com-posers, and before interest in it was reawakened. Schooled in the older motet style and tradition, cantors were often found among those least in sympathy with the lied, while organists tended to pride themselves on being more up to date in their taste. Schein is a notable exception, but his contribution belongs to an early and transitional stage.

When the Thirty Years War ended in 1648, Bach was not yet born, but by this time the first phase in the development of baroque poetry (and of the lied) was over. Its predominant theme, the vanity of the world, reflected the experience of war and pestilence, but also, in more complex ways, the awesome sense of princely power *sub specie aeternitatis*, trailing the reflected glory of infinite and divine reality, 'from everlasting . . . to endless years the same',

> . . . the figure of God's majesty,
> His captain, steward, deputy elect.

In the formal concentration of compact forms like the sonnet, when human existence is being dealt with in relation to God and eternity,

---

[1] G. F. Hartlaub, 'Die Musik im Generalbaßzeitalter', *Deutsche Vierteljahrschrift für Literaturwissenschaft und Geistesgeschichte*, xvi, 1938, p. 209.

[2] *Ausführlicher Bericht vom Gebrauche der Con- und Dissonantien*, ch. xiii, sec. 4.

[3] Briefly, of the songs sometimes attributed to Bach (as in Schemelli's *Musicalisches Gesang-Buch*, Leipzig, 1736, and the second *Anna Magdalena Notenbuch*) relatively few are definitely by him. For full details cf. W. Schmiederer (ed.), *Thematisch-Systematisches Verzeichnis der musikalischen Werke von J. S. Bach*, Leipzig, 1950.

to a reality beyond the whims of change, there is often, as in fugue, a dominant and unifying theme, to which the poem returns at its conclusion, as if beyond this no development can be conceived as possible, and in intervening episodes the poet attempts to establish a relationship with spheres so far removed from mortal man that only metaphorical explanation is possible. Just as *le style continu*[1] was not the musical idiom of song, poetry of this sort did not appeal to the lied composers, and notably in the case of Gryphius, who wrote much poetry of this exalted kind, they preferred his more homely and discursive strophic verse.

Though the baroque was a courtly age, the epithet does not define all aspects of its culture, and there is even much to be said for the idea of the 'antinomy of courtly and anti-courtly' as its central axis.[2] The aristocratic world, even in a simple geographical sense, was never far away, providing influential criteria of taste and expression. But there were important centres of culture, like Hamburg and Leipzig, without a court, though their administration was oligarchical, and here and elsewhere, as at Königsberg, was to be found a great deal of poetry with a different stamp. Even folk-song enjoyed quite a vigorous existence, as in the *Venus-Gärtlein: Oder Viel Schöne, auserlesene Weltliche Lieder* (1656), though not uninfluenced by prevailing conventions.

Poetry, in fact, spoke with two voices. With its public voice it proclaimed exalted truths about existence, about the majesty of God and the death of kings. With its private voice it sang of homelier themes, of everyday joys and sorrows, of love true and false. Often a single poet would have both at his command, like Paul Fleming. There is no need to assume that the writing of both types of poetry by one writer arose from mere pretence, since criteria of sincerity in poetry in the seventeenth century were different from those of the nineteenth. Some light is thrown by Caspar Stieler's *Der allzeitfertige Secretarius* (1680), a set of instructions on how to write letters. The gist is that letters to people of different class and occupation demand a style corresponding to a person's station in what was a rigorously stratified society. The problem is clarified by reference to Simon Dach, who in co-operation with Heinrich Albert is important in a central phase of the baroque lied. Two posthumous collections[3] of his verse published in the

[1] The phrase is taken from A. Hoérée, *Albert Roussel*, Paris, 1938, p. 76.
[2] E. Lunding, 'German Baroque Literature: A Synthetic View', *German Life and Letters*, iii, 1949, p. 3.
[3] *Chur-Brandenburgische Rose | Adler | Löw und Scepter*, published by his widow and dedicated to Friedrich Wilhelm, Markgraf of Brandenburg, and *Poetische Wercke, Bestehend in Heroischen Gedichten, Denen beygefüget zwey seiner verfertigten Poetischen Schauspiele*, Königsberg, 1696.

seventeenth century significantly isolated his more ceremonial verse, one of them describing the poems as 'heroic' because 'for the most part they are dedicated to high personages'. Some poetry he wrote he himself never published, because it lacked the ceremonial qualities obligatory in high-flown public utterance—and it was in poetry of this kind that the baroque continuo lied found its textual basis.

The term denotes solo song, generally strophic and usually built upon a figured bass, in the realization of which a good deal was left to the discretion of the performer within the rules laid down. This was a new type of vocal music, related to attitudes and experience different from those embodied in the earlier vocal polyphony, and the disintegration of this was the necessary preliminary to the creation of the continuo lied.

# PART I

‹‹‹··››› ‹‹‹··››› ‹‹‹··››› ‹‹‹··››› ‹‹‹··››› ‹‹‹··››› ‹‹‹··››› ‹‹‹··››› ‹‹‹··››› ‹‹‹··››› ‹‹‹··››› ‹‹‹··››› ‹‹‹··›››

## I

## *The Older German Texts and Polyphony*

THREE considerable collections of polyphonic settings of German texts survive from the second half of the fifteenth century, the *Lochamer Liederbuch*, the *Schedelsches Liederbuch*, and the *Glogauer Liederbuch*, the most important of them, which dates from about 1480. The pieces range from Latin numbers to dance-like *chansons*, but the most characteristic type is the *Tenorlied*, in which the polyphonic structure is organized upon the tenor. This acquired a special importance in Germany, where it showed signs of establishing an independent tradition. The *cantus fermus* originated in liturgical music where, as in the masses of Dufay and Dunstable, it was entrusted with the enunciation of the dogmatic principles of the faith. The association of polyphonic vocal music with popular and even folk-song elements, as particularly in the *Glogauer Liederbuch*, was a development out of keeping with the original conception of the *cantus fermus*. But this remained a serviceable principle of musical organization when its liturgical origins had ceased to matter.

Important features of the *Tenorlied* are illustrated in Heinrich Finck who, born about the middle of the fifteenth century, entered the service of Duke Ulrich of Stuttgart, became *Kapellmeister* at Salzburg Cathedral, and later served the court at Vienna. He was a contemporary of Paul Hofhaimer, organist to Archbishop Sigmund at Innsbruck and a court musician under Emperor Maximilian I. The texts of his secular songs show the impact of Renaissance humanism, and the character of the words influences their use of the *cantus fermus* technique. In most of them the tune is still in the tenor, but it seems often to have been the composer's free invention. To a greater degree than with most of his contemporaries the other parts are more than merely subsidiary to the tenor; sometimes even the upper part is at least as

B

important. Like Finck, Hofhaimer exemplifies the rather rigid style of composition common in the *Tenorlied*, but in his case, too, parts other than the tenor tend to share its importance. The changing character of polyphonic vocal music in Germany by the first decade or two of the sixteenth century is felt also in the work of the Flemish composer Heinrich Isaak who, after service under Lorenzo de' Medici and Maximilian I, died in Innsbruck in 1517. His music embraces conservative examples of the *Tenorlied* and also pieces more modern in conception, like his homophonic frottolas. His well-known setting of *Innsbruck, ich muß dich lassen* is homophonic, with the tune in the upper part—but his earlier and less-familiar setting of the same text is consistently polyphonic.

German *cantus fermus* polyphony reached its fruition in the work of Ludwig Senfl, another of Maximilian I's musicians and for some
Ex. 1 years attached to the Bavarian court. The melody of *Geduld um Huld* is in the tenor, but it is not monopolized by it, and the contrapuntal pattern at the beginning is soon modified by a lyrical and flexible intertwining of the parts. As in many *Tenorlieder*, the tenor tune is rather disjointed, but in other parts it is shaped into a more flowing line. Adrianus Coclicus classified Senfl, in the *Compendium Musices* (1552), as a leading exponent among the 'moderns' of the art of *musica reservata*, expressive music. This is not surprising, for in some of his pieces his pictorialism foreshadows the Renaissance madrigal, as in the treatment of 'flowing' in *Die Brünnlein, die da fließen*, but its limits are seen in the way the same figure is also associated with words for which it is not particularly appropriate.

Senfl probably died about 1556, the year in which there appeared the fifth and final part of the collection compiled by Georg Forster under the title *Frische teutsche Liedlein*. Eleven years later Orlando di Lasso published his first settings of German songs, *Newe teütsche Liedlein*. Born in Mons in 1532, Lasso served as a youth under Ferdinand Gonzaga in Sicily, but in 1556 he settled in Munich where, having been knighted by Maximilian II, he died in the service of the Bavarian court in 1594. Lasso's contribution to German song, decisively influenced by his experience of Italian music, was of crucial significance, and following Burmeister's praise (in the *Musica Poetica*)[1] of his expressive use of figures, theoreticians of the seventeenth and eighteenth century respected him above all for his ability to convey the feeling of his texts; Mattheson mentions him in this sense in the

[1] pp. 74 seq.

*Critica Musica.*[1] His knowledge of German was very limited, but his impact on the traditional German *Tenorlied* was profound and far-reaching.

Lasso's *Newe teütsche Liedlein*, dedicated to Duke Wilhelm IV of Bavaria (son of Albrecht IV) and published in Munich, were influenced by Senfl and Forster, both musically and in the choice of texts. But the way the different parts are allowed to contribute to the *cantus fermus* and the unwillingness to let this be bound by a caesura at the end of lines, together with madrigalian touches coloured by his knowledge of Italian poetry, produce features that are markedly modern in effect as compared with Forster. In his next collection, the second part of the *Newe teütsche Lieder* in 1572, the handling of the *cantus fermus* tends to be more conservative, but other features, like the more madrigalian relationship of the parts, derive from another tradition and point in a different direction. When the third part appeared in 1576, Lasso in his foreword asked his patron (Duke Ernst of Bavaria, son of Duke Albrecht V), remembering the 'Italian sweetness' (*italianische lieblichkeit*) in his work so far, not to be dismayed by the German 'uncouthness' (*teutsche Dapffrigkeit*) of the new pieces. It is true that Lasso here handles the *cantus fermus* in rather a rigid fashion, but it is not clear why, having already accommodated himself to some of the 'uncouth' German habits, he should at this stage feel it necessary to apologize. There may have been opportunist reasons of a political kind,[2] and he may have been influenced by the growth meanwhile of his reputation as a madrigalist. Even so, the expressive resources of these pieces, their chromaticism and use of repetition to heighten feeling, exceed the normal scope of vocal polyphony within the native German tradition.

It would be an over-simplification to say of German vocal polyphony that its tendency had been to regard the words as merely incidental, but they were certainly not always a main concern, and to an extent that by mature baroque standards was severely criticized by Caspar Printz in his *Historische Beschreibung der Edelen Sing- und Kling-Kunst* (1690). The composers of the sixteenth century, Printz wrote rather ungenerously, 'paid more attention to the music than to the text, made the music first and then tacked the words on to it, causing such confusion and distortion . . .'.[3] The use of vocal music as *Tafelmusik*

---

[1] ii, 1725, p. 377.
[2] Cf. W. Boetticher, *Orlando di Lasso und seine Zeit*, Cassel and Basel, 1958, p. 511.
[3] p. 132.

probably detracted from the incentive to regard them exclusively as songs, and from about 1550 instruments were increasingly used with voices in *Tafelmusik*. The combination of voice and instruments could, of course, be thought of for purely domestic music-making, but in Germany the frequent use of instruments like bombards, shawms, crumhorns, cornetts, and trombones suggests the resources of municipal and court bands. Senfl's influence in Munich may have encouraged this practice, where his vocal music was sometimes even performed on instruments alone. The sub-title of Lasso's *Newe teütsche Lieder* describes them as pieces 'that can not only be sweetly sung but can also be performed on all sorts of instruments', though, with the expressive treatment of his texts, he would hardly have regarded instrumental performance as ideal, and this was a conventional sort of title anyway. Georg Forster was quite frank about it in a preface in 1539: 'Since, however, we have printed these songs not for the sake of the text but of the music, in the case of songs where no text was available we have provided words in order that they might not lack a text.' It could easily happen too that in polyphonic music the words were obscured by the movement of the parts, though they were often so familiar as to reduce the need to hear them clearly.

Lasso's readiness, despite his knowledge of poetry of a different kind, his proven skill in setting it to music, and despite (or because of) his rudimentary knowledge of the German language, to use traditional German texts of the kind associated with the *Tenorlied*, reflects their established place at the time in German taste, and the same applies to his utilization of the musical features. But the way he handled this form under Italian influence brought pressure to bear on the shape of the texts. His application of madrigalian features to his German songs made the strophic structure of the older German *Gesellschaftslied* almost unrecognizable. Since he did not feel bound rigidly to adhere to the *cantus fermus* nor to bind his texts inflexibly to it, his settings have something of the character of an improvised succession of separate motifs. This procedure, which has links with Italian poetry, was used by him most conspicuously in the 1567 set. In addition, many of his songs depart from the strophic structure usual in most German vocal music of the time, and point in the direction of through-composition in the style of the madrigal.[1]

In short, Lasso had led the *Tenorlied* to its highest point of development, less, however, by adding anything new than by developing

[1] Cf. Boetticher, op. cit., p. 328.

features already apparent in some of the more subtle examples of the form, and in the process he had contributed towards loosening its structure, undermining its tradition, and weakening its hold. At the same time the *Tenorlied* was coming under pressure from competing forms of romance origin. Lasso's work includes examples of the homophonic *chanson* and also of the *villanella*, and the latter particularly helped to suggest possibilities beyond the *Tenorlied*.

Homophonic, dispensing with textual repetition, and with clearcut rhythmic divisions, the villanella had always had a popular flavour. Gregor Lange remarked in connexion with his *Newe deudsche Lieder mit dreyen Stimmen* (Breslau, 1584) that the singing of villanellas helped one 'to enjoy oneself . . . in merry gatherings'. Michael Praetorius recognized the simple origins of the villanella when in the *Syntagma Musicum* he grouped it among the songs of peasants and artisans— 'ein Bawrliedlein welche die Bawren vnd gemeine Handwercksleute singen . . . eine Bäwrisch Music zu einer Bäwrischen Matery'.[1] Zacconi in the *Prattica di musica* (Venice, 1592) associated it with peasant girls singing in the fields, and in the second half of the eighteenth century Klopstock, quoting one of Regnart's villanellas that he had found reprinted in Paul von der Aelst's *Blum und Ausbund Allerhandt Auserlesener Weltlicher Züchtiger Lieder und Rheymen* (1602), still recalled its humble beginnings by referring to this collection as a 'set of simple artisan songs'.[2] Nevertheless, in the course of the sixteenth century the villanella established itself as an art form intended for the same people as enjoyed the madrigal and it gained an equivalent prestige.

From the musical point of view the villanella is of particular significance in this context in that, popularized by Regnart, in the hands of Schein and Nauwach it was to provide the basis for the critical transition from part-music to continuo lied. Regnart, however, was not only a composer. He was also a poet and one able, under the refining influence of modish Italian texts familiar to him as a musician, to write elegant and polished verse. This was important at a time when there was no poetry in Germany independent of music and when, apart from folk-song, much of it, most notoriously the texts of the *Meistergesang*, was crude and ungainly. The verse of Regnart's villanellas may make a different impression without the music, but,

[1] iii, pt. 1, ch. vii.
[2] 'Von deutscher Art und Kunst', Bibliographisches Institut edition of Klopstock's *Werke*, ii. 49.

if the music had vanished and its existence had been forgotten, no one reading the poetry would have been conscious of the loss.

Poetry of this kind and quality was hardly worth the trouble of writing if in performance it was to be obscured, and its elegant symmetry interfered with, by the rambling and intertwining lines of a polyphonic setting. Lasso had been able to accept the form of the *Tenorlied* only because, in using it, he had accepted texts of the older kind. Regnart's texts, however, encouraged, even demanded, a different musical approach, simpler and more up to date, even though as yet music could only offer him the resources of part-music. The creation of sophisticated verse of this sort was bound to present in the partnership of music and poetry a problem that could not be solved immediately, but meanwhile Regnart made good use of the opportunities available by uniting it with a musical form with the simplest possible relations between the parts, and he effectively exploited the dual association of the villanella, the peculiar mixture of naïvety and sophistication that it allowed.

# II

## *Music and the Beginnings of the New Poetry*

### (i) JAKOB REGNART AND THE VILLANELLA

REGNART's *Kurtzweilige teutsche Lieder* appeared in 1567, 1577, and 1579, and a complete edition of sixty-seven pieces in 1583. Described in the sub-title as 'in the manner of the Neapolitan or Italian villanella', they enjoyed greater popularity than any other vocal music published in Germany at this time. His five-part songs of 1580 in madrigalian style had nothing like the same success. When the *Kurtzweilige teutsche Lieder* began to appear, Regnart was probably in his late twenties. He died around the turn of the century after spending most of his life at various courts and the years 1568–70 in Italy.

His adherence to Italian models in his texts is illustrated by comparing the following, first encountered in a setting by Vecchi, with Regnart's version:

> Chi vuol veder un bosco folto et spesso,
> Venga a mirar il mio misero core
> Quante saette ci ha tirato Amore.

> Chi vuol veder duo fonti d'aqua viva,
> Venga a veder questi occhi egri e dolenti,
> Ch'amor gli ha fatti duo fiumi correnti.

> Chi vuol veder come arde una fornace,
> Venga a veder me sol ch'in ogni loco
> Amor m'ha fatto tutto fiamma e foco.

> Chi vuol saper di questo la cagione,
> Miri costei che sua rara beltade
> M'infiamma ogn'hore e in lei non è piètade.


> Wer sehen will zween lebendige Brunnen,
> Der soll mein zwei betrübte Augen sehen,
> Die mir vor Weinen schier seind ausgerunnen.

> Wer sehen will viel groß und tiefe Wunden,
> Der soll mein sehr verwundtes Herz besehen,
> Also hat's Lieb versehret oben und unten.

> Wer sehen will ein Brunst groß ungeheur,
> Der soll allein mich armen Mann besehen;
> Denn ich brenn ganz und gar von Liebesfeuer.
>
> Wer wissen will, wer mir auftu solch Plagen,
> Soll nach der Schönsten auf der Erden fragen,
> Sie ist allein Ursach all meiner Klagen.

This poem, in which Regnart rearranges the order of the first two stanzas, became popular enough for a version to be included by Paul Kauffmann in his villanellas of 1614, *Allerley Kurtzweilige Teutsche Liedlein mit dreyen Stimmen*, in which more than forty pieces are from Regnart, with others from Lechner, Ivo de Vento, and Brechtel. Demantius had already used some of Regnart's villanellas with modifications in his *Neue Teutsche Weltliche Lieder* (1595) and so too had Paul von der Aelst in his *Blum und Ausbund Allerhandt Auserlesener Weltlicher Züchtiger Lieder und Rheymen* (1602). With slight changes the first two verses of this particular text constitute one item in the early nineteenth-century folk-song collection *Des Knaben Wunderhorn*.[1] It demonstrates the pattern followed in one type of Regnart's villanellas, three-line stanzas rhyming *aaa*, *aba*, or *abb*, each line usually having eleven syllables. A different variety, comprising six-line stanzas with six or seven syllables to a line and rhyming *aabbcc*, is illustrated by the poem beginning:

> Venus du und dein Kind
> Seid alle beide blind
> Und pflegt sich zu verblenden
> Wer sich zu euch tut wenden,
> Wie ichs wohl hab erfahren
> In meinen jungen Jahren.

This too figures in Kauffmann's collection, and well into the seventeenth century Khuen, for example, uses a bit of it in the *Marianum Epithalamium*:

> Gar schmählich dies empfind
> Die Venus und ihr Kind.

This poetry combines the characteristic artifice of much baroque verse with regular line-units demanded by the music, and, foreshadowing the strophic songs of the seventeenth century, a neat succession of identically patterned stanzas. The mixture of sophisti-

---

[1] iii, no. 6. No. 8 in the same volume (*Der süße Schlaf, der sonst stillt alles wohl*) is a slightly modified version of the text quoted by Klopstock, referred to on p. 5.

cation in theme and metaphor with the polish of its verse-form and prosody, which justifies its existence as poetry independent of music, is also illustrated in this example:

> Mein Mund der singt, mein Herz vor Trauern weint,
> So böslich sind mein Mund und Herz vereint.
> Daß solchs konnt sein, hätt ich niemals gemeint.
>
> Mit Singen ich gleichwohl mein Zeit vertreib,
> Daneben doch in Langweil allzeit bleib,
> Das schaffet alls ein Adeliches Weib.
>
> Dann daß die nit mag widerfahren mir,
> Nach deren strebt mein Herz, Mut und Begier,
> Das möchte mich von Sinnen bringen schier.
>
> Ich glaub, daß ich dazu geboren sei,
> Daß ich von Lieb mag nimmer leben frei,
> So ich doch nichts als Elend hab dabei.

The self-conscious elegance of this poem can be appreciated if we compare it with a song on a similar theme (*Mein Mund wohl fröhlich singet*), but with a more native metre and extended to fourteen verses, in the *Zwey schöne Liederlein* published at Magdeburg in 1600, or with a more traditional kind of verse obviously derived from it in Moscherosch's novel *Wunderliche und wahrhafftige Gesichte Philanders von Sittewald* (1613):

> traurig sein und doch singen,
> ist ein traurig Pein,
> es läßt sich schwerlich zwingen
> reimen und lustig sein.

Laughter and tears intermingle in the unpremeditated moods of folk-song, but in Regnart's poem the contradiction is reflected upon and reasoned about. It relies for its effect largely on sophisticated use of antithesis (the mouth sings, the heart weeps, and so forth), the central antithesis being the idea that love causes pain. It is the very self-conscious way in which Regnart exploits this principle that gives his verse its up-to-date and modish character.

There is a pretence of a different kind in the music where, with an obviously deliberate disregard for the musical proprieties, parallel fifths—a traditional feature of the villanella—impart a naïvety in striking contrast with the sophistication of the texts, and in contrast too with touches suggestive of madrigal composition, like the little melisma in the upper part at *singt*, and the way repetition of the phrase

Ex. 2

*mein Herz vor Trauern* points the affective implication of the words.
Ex. 3 Affective use of imitation is found in another piece, in which the
phrase *will mir vor Leid* appears three times, each time a third lower.
The effect is then enhanced at the last appearance by the way the
upper part, followed by the second and third in partial imitation,
continues with a rising and then a falling melismatic figure at *Leid*.

One way of appreciating the peculiar outcome of this union of
seeming naïvety and artifice is to compare the originals with Lechner's
five-part arrangement of some of them as madrigals in 1579, where
only the artifice remains. While Regnart's verse has independent
qualities as poetry, the music qualifies, or comments on, its sophistication, and without the words the music is flat and uninteresting.
Regnart,. however, was by no means unique in these respects, as one
can see, for example, by reference to Nola, whose *Canzoni Villanesche*
(1541) acquired such celebrity as to make it reasonable to surmise
that Regnart knew these pieces and may well have been affected by them.
Like a number of other Italian composers, Nola was not averse to
parodying the madrigal in the humbler guise of the villanella, a fairly
widespread custom at this time. One writer discusses Nola's *Madonna,*
*voi me fare* in connexion with the practice of using the villanella to
raise a smile at the pretensions of the madrigal: 'Lines might be
borrowed from older poems, or exaggerated texts or inappropriate
musical settings might be used for the sake of caricature. In this . . .
the opening words are repeated several times, set in dignified style,
and then reach the not very exalted conclusion, "una camisa, madonna,
voi me fare", with parallel fifths on the first three syllables.'[1] Another
critic said in 1938[2] of Regnart's parodistic tendency that the madrigal
is here 'pulled down from its pedestal and dressed with the attributes
of a section of society used to vigorous and natural feeling. The
Gentiluomo and his Donna are, so to speak, asked to slip into peasant
costume in order to become aware of their remoteness from nature and
reality.' This, however, goes too far, and Regnart's motives were more
playful and his intentions less deliberate than this might suggest.

At all events, poetry such as this, self-conscious in its artifice and
inviting admiration for the novelty of technical skill and polish,
wished to be heard and understood. One did not write this sort of
verse for it to be lost in a maze of polyphony. The parts almost always
move together, and the upper part has the tune. But the melody does

---

[1] G. Reese, *Music in the Renaissance*, London, 1954, p. 333.
[2] H. Osthoff, *Die Niederländer und das deutsche Lied*, Berlin, 1938, pp. 367–8.

not attract the main interest, and, since it has a simple chordal relationship to the other parts, its freedom of movement and of expression is very limited. Though Regnart's settings are radically different from the extreme experiments in monody of the Italian Renaissance by men anxious that the words should not be obscured by polyphonic elaboration, Count Bardi's views have a bearing in this context. Our composers, Bardi wrote, would consider it 'a mortal sin if all the parts were heard to beat at the same time with the same notes, with the same syllables of the verse, and with the same longs and shorts; the more they make the parts move, the more artful they think they are'.[1] In the *Kurtzweilige teutsche Lieder* nothing remains of the vocal polyphonic tradition.

The complexities of polyphony were also being resisted by those who attached importance to the special idea of measured music, based on the additive rhythms of Greek verse. They practised the theory, which they believed to have been the basis of Greek music, that a short syllable should be set to a short note and a syllable twice as long to a longer note. Early in the sixteenth century Petrus Tritonius had illustrated this notion in his settings of Horace (*Melopoiae sive harmonia*, 1507), influenced by the Bavarian humanist Conrad Celtis, and both Senfl (*Varia carminum genera*, 1534) and Hofhaimer (*Harmoniae poëticae*, 1539) experimented with the idea. In France, in close association with Baïf's Academy of Poetry, it led to the *Pseaumes en vers mezurez mis en musique* of Claude Lejeune, who died, probably in the same year as Regnart, in 1600. This theory proved unfruitful in the long run, but it had important short-term consequences for part-music. For the result is a 'syllabic harmony' and a *rythme d'ensemble* alien to polyphony, since the determination 'to preserve the metre in the ensemble' necessitates each voice singing each syllable simultaneously.[2] Regnart must have known about these experiments, if only through the interest of his brother, in Ronsard's poetry, which François Regnart set to music in four and five parts in 1575 (*Poésies de P. de Ronsard & autres Poëtes*, Douai, 1575). In the *Kurtzweilige teutsche Lieder* the voices do not move together with absolute consistency, but they do so most of the time, and the term *rythme d'ensemble* usefully characterizes this aspect of them. Some lines, moreover, come close to the effect of measured music, the reason being that the texts are close copies, in a stressed language, of Italian

[1] O. Strunk (ed.), *Source Readings in Music History*, London, 1952, p. 294.
[2] F. A. Yates, *The French Academies of the Sixteenth Century*, London, 1947, p. 57.

models in which not stress but the counting of syllables determines
the prosody. Sometimes Regnart's verse depends to such an extent
on the number of syllables that it can hardly be scanned accen-
tually:

> Wer sehen will zween lebendige Brunnen.

But a line like:

> Der soll mein zwei betrübte Augen sehen

is strictly iambic, and in a good number of Regnart's villanellas
such lines predominate, illustrating the point that music 'is of such
fundamental importance for the development of lyrical strophic forms
that an historical account of their development would only be possible
in connexion with the history of music'.[1]

It has long been recognized that the metrical orderliness of Regnart's
verse owes much to music: 'The influence of the melody makes him
pay attention to prosody and rhythm, and he tries as far as possible to
make the natural emphasis of the words fit the metre.'[2] Of the factors
combining to produce this result, one is the part played by additive
rhythms, creating lines of equal length through adherence to a given
number of syllables to each line. Another is the regular accentuation
in the stressed dance-rhythm of the music, and this gives to many of
Regnart's lines metrical features anticipating the reforms of Opitz.

Contemporaneously with Regnart, the effect of musical rhythms
on poetry can be studied in the interesting transitional figure of
Theobald Hoeck, whose *Schönes Blumenfeldt* was published in 1601.
Much of Hoeck's verse is marred by an ungainliness stamped with the
influence of *Meistergesang*, but some shows a more careful sense of
metrical order, though at the cost of awkward elisions and, as in this
borrowing from Regnart, of a final line that obviously had to be strait-
laced into the iambic pattern:

> Jetzt bin ich einmal frei
> Von Lieb und Liebesbanden,
> Kein Lieb ist mehr vorhanden,
> D'Lieb hab ich überstanden.

Often the metrically tidiest parts of Hoeck's poems are the *fa-la-la*
refrains, influenced by Italian dance-forms, notably the *balletto* with
its clear alternation of stressed and unstressed beats.

[1] F. Kauffmann, *Deutsche Metrik nach ihrer geschichtlichen Entwicklung*, Marburg, 1897,
p. 136.     [2] W. Stammler, *Von der Mystik zum Barock*, Stuttgart, 1927, p. 451.

In Regnart's verse what tended to lead in the direction of regular accentuation was the effect of a *rythme d'ensemble*, associated with mensural music, on a stressed language, even though the prosody of his models depended on the counting of syllables. The success of the *Kurtzweilige teutsche Lieder* could therefore tempt one, justifiably to some extent perhaps, to include it among the factors that helped to prepare the ground for Opitz's reforms, especially in view of the increasing popularity of the villanella in Germany. Regnart's success contributed to this; also, villanellas were easy to compose, provided a simple pattern to follow, and lent themselves to straightforward arrangements for the most popular of instruments, the lute. But in the hands of Regnart's immediate successors and imitators the texts lost their close connexion with Italian models. Traditional German features, even folk-song influences, were absorbed, and some of the later villanellas did little more than adapt texts similar to Forster's, Regnart's metre sometimes sharing a stanza with lines of obviously earlier origin. Older poetic forms were forced into the musical pattern of the villanella, often doing violence to the text. And meanwhile a new wave of Italian influence diverted interest to the canzonet.

# III

## Music and the Beginnings of the New Poetry
### (ii) HANS LEO HASSLER AND THE CANZONET

THE *Canzonette* of 1590 with Italian texts was Hassler's first published work. Six years later he demonstrated his powers of expressive polyphony in a set of Italian madrigals. In the same year appeared his *Neüe teütsche gesang nach art der Welschen Madrigalian vn Canzonetten*, which have some contrapuntal features, but are mainly homophonic and are divided into clearly defined sections. Few of them are really madrigals, most are best described as canzonets. But this is a vague term, indicating no more than a chordal setting in two or three parts of a light and as a rule strophic poem—'little short songs . . . with secular texts' was Praetorius's definition.[1]

Regnart was a Netherlander, Hassler a German—the first important German composer, in fact, to make the Italian journey. Born in Nuremberg in 1564, he spent a year in Italy, where he studied under Andrea Gabrieli, organist at St. Mark's. He left Venice in 1585 and, though a Protestant, entered the service of the Fuggers, in which he enjoyed an assured existence and the encouragement of a wealthy patron keenly interested in music and the arts. His usefulness to the Fuggers was not limited to music. He and his two brothers had connexions with mining and the silver trade, and he pursued his financial affairs with vigorous enthusiasm. He organized loans on behalf of the Fuggers and of the Emperor, and his merits as a musician need not have been the only factor in his ennoblement by Rudolf II in 1595. In 1601 he moved to Nuremberg, in 1604 to Ulm, where he married a merchant's daughter. In 1608 he settled in Dresden as musician at the court of Elector Christian II. He accompanied the court of Johann Georg of Saxony, recently elevated to Elector, to Frankfurt for the election of Emperor Matthias, and died there in 1612. At home in cultivated company, elegant and self-confident, he was a characteristic Renaissance figure, of restless energy and combining art with an adventurous zest for practical activity.

[1] *Syntagma Musicum*, iii, pt. 1, ch. iv.

Hassler's Italian experience was decisive for his music, but one must not overlook the influence of more traditional elements which, despite Italian encroachments, were still alive in Nuremberg. Forster had lived there till 1544 and there published the last two volumes of his collection, and in Hassler's youth church music in Nuremberg must have consisted largely of polyphonic music by leading Netherland and German composers. Commerce, however, was strengthening Nuremberg's links with Italy, and Italian music too was winning favour. Lechner, thanks to whom to a great extent Lasso's music had made its mark there, left Nuremberg only in the year that Hassler went to Venice, and Italian music also had a keen protagonist in the cantor Friedrich Lindner, who during Hassler's time in Nuremberg was busy collecting and performing works by Italian masters, and Hassler knew him well.

The texts of Hassler's *Neüe teütsche gesang* are German, but so closely imitated from the Italian as to make his claim in the dedication to have composed both words and music a bit of an exaggeration. In style and conception, however, they are less uniform than their Italian derivation might suggest. One opens with lines clearly betraying Italian influence:

> Jungfrau, dein schöne Gestalt
> Erfreut mich sehr, je länger je mehr,

but it ends with an echo of German folk-song:

> Ich bin dein, du bist mein,
> Nichts soll uns widerstreben
> Im Leben, merk eben.

Phrases like *O Adeliche Zier, Liebesbrunst* have the Italian stamp, and the strained use of words in this example:

> Falsch Lieb, warum mich fliehest?
> G'fällt dir dann so wohl mein Sterben und Schmertze?
> Bist du doch je mein Hertze?
> Meinst durch dein Fliehen eben,
> Falsch Lieb, mir nehmens Leben?
> Ach, niemand sterben kann, der nicht leidt Schmertze,
> Und kein Schmertze leiden kann, wer hat kein Hertze,

results from slavish imitation of a madrigal of Guarini. But the following is characteristically German and even recalls the older *Bar*-form:

> Ich scheid von dir mit Leide,
> Verlaß dich mein treus Hertze,
> Das bringt mir großen Schmertze.

Ach weh vor Leid ich stirbe,
Kanns dann nicht anders sein, was soll ich tun?
O wie ein schweres Leiden
Noch muß es sein gescheiden,
Vor Angst ich gar verdirbe,
Ach weh, ich scheid und stirbe.

More significant than such vestiges of earlier tradition are pieces with a text wholly in the Italian style:

Mein Lieb will mit mir kriegen,
Hat sich gerüst zur Schlacht,
Läßt ihren Fahnen fliegen,
Trotzt auf ihr große Macht,
Vermeint, ich soll sie fliehen,
Hab Liebskrieg nie versucht:
Gegn ihr will ich auch ziehen,
Sie jagen g'schwind in d'Flucht.
Frisch her, tu tapfer schießen
Mit deim vergiften Pfeil,
Dein Hochmut will ich büßen
Gar bald in schneller Eil.
Diri diri diridon.
Schieß zu, nur g'schwind daran.
Ach weh, ich bin durchschossen
Mit ihren Äuglein zart,
Viel Blut hab ich vergossen,
Tödlich verwundet hart.
O Lieb, ich tu mich geben
Dir auf die Gnade dein,
Ich bitt, schenk mir das Leben,
Dein G'fangener will ich sein.

The scorned lover, dramatizing his plight, affects the poses of valour, indignation, and finally surrender. He has never before essayed a 'war against love', *Liebskrieg*—a coined word, a modish conceit. But he resolves to resist, and challenges love to do its worst. He is struck down, not by his beloved's arrow, but by her tender eyes. Wounded and bleeding, he pleads for mercy and life. He had taken up arms to defend his freedom merely to discover that he can live only as love's prisoner. In this exhibition we are required to appreciate the self-assurance that allows the poet the extravagance of pretending that he could be forced into so abject a surrender, and also to admire the artistic ingenuity with which he builds his edifice of wit out of the fashionable learning of his day.

Ex. 4    Antiphonal music, a Renaissance discovery and much practised at

St. Mark's, is exciting and exhilarating in its sheer joy of sound, and here the two choirs add a rousing, sensuous pleasure to the drama of the text. They unite at bar 19 to reinforce the resolve to take up arms and scatter the beloved's forces, combine again at bar 42, and for a third time at the passionate plea:

> Ich bitt, schenk mir das Leben.

The music is firmly based on a tonic-dominant structure, and the only features that might be regarded as archaic are a suggestion of modality and the plagal cadence at the end. But by the standards of the Italian madrigalists, who would have provided some of his daily fare in Venice, Hassler is restrained in his use of the more affective devices. Chromaticism, sparingly used as a rule in all Hassler's secular music, occurs here only at bar 82, where, as the lover is pierced by his lady's eyes and the *weh* is repeated, a stock Italian progression introduces a chromatic alteration into the original G major chord. But firm tonality is quickly restored with an A major chord at bar 83 and the C major cadence three bars later. After the short episode in D minor (*Äuglein zart*), the tonal pattern is slightly disturbed with the movement towards A minor around bars 93–94, and the suspended seventh at bar 96 momentarily blurs the tonality, as the lover is struck down. However, after a fleeting impression of modality at bar 99 (where D minor would be implied but for the B natural in the third chord), the dominant is established by bar 101 and tonal order fully restored by return to the tonic by bar 106.

Music of a more extravagant kind might well have been expected in view of the affective opportunities offered by the text. Hassler's motet *Ad Dominum cum tribularer*, for example, shows that the means were at his disposal, though it is the 'only one of all Hassler's motets in which he makes full use of chromaticism'.[1] In *Mein Lieb will mit mir kriegen* he seems, as always in the *Neüe teütsche gesang*, deliberately to have avoided emotional extravagance. One restraining factor was Hassler's Protestantism, and this is reflected in the chorale-like element in some of his texts. On first impression, for example, parts of the following read more like a hymn than a love-song:

> O Aufenthalt meins Lebens,
> Ich bitt, tu mir Hilf geben,
> Nimm hin, hab dir mein Hertze,
> Welches durch dich stets leid groß Angst und Schmertze.

---

[1] Anna Amalie Abert, *Die stilistischen Voraussetzungen der 'Cantiones sacrae' von Heinrich Schütz*, Wolfenbüttel and Berlin, 1935, p. 132.

Laß mich doch nicht verderben,
Noch gar verzweifelt sterben,
Tu mich wieder erquicken
Mit dein schön Äuglein klar lieblich anblicken.

Hilf mir aus meinem Leiden,
Tu dich nicht von mir scheiden,
Gib mir auch dein treus Hertze,
Zu Freud und Schertz verkehr mein Angst und Schmertze.

How closely he could identify himself with the German Protestant mood is seen in his four-part *Psalmen vnd christliche Gesäng* of 1607, which are far removed from the sensuous excitements of Venetian Renaissance music. When the texts of the *Neüe teütsche gesang* were adapted as religious songs, the result was revealingly suggestive of the chorale. After all, his formative environment had been in the first place the patrician life of Nuremberg with its emphasis on the staid moral values and its distrust of extremes. These were commonly regarded as natural characteristics of light-hearted Italians, who were often seen in the town and to whom any moral disturbance tended to be attributed. German composers in Nuremberg, moreover, felt a bond between themselves and the city's institutions, and works would not infrequently be dedicated to the council or some representative citizen—as in the case of Ott's masses of 1539 and Lechner's *Newe teutsche Lieder* (1576). The latter, believing that 'secular songs also benefit the cause of the noble art of music provided that the *fines verecundiae* are not overstepped', only ventured to dedicate them to a person in authority because they 'do not contain irresponsible excesses or anything shameful or vicious such as might offend moral honour'. Lasso acted likewise with his *Newe teütsche Liedlein* and later with the *Newe teutsche vnd etliche frantzösische Gesäng*, but it was in Italy that he always published his madrigals. A Protestant, Hassler's masses were composed for Catholic worship, and it was in his church music that the more affective aspects of Italian music were most apparent.

Like his texts, the music of the *Neüe teütsche gesang* is far from uniform in style, and the circumstances make this not very surprising. One illustration of the interplay of different styles in Hassler's time would be Lechner's *Newe teutsche Lieder*, in which 'may be found archaic *Tenorlieder* (based on liturgic *canti fermi*) . . . cheek by jowl with modern Italianate madrigals and villanelle'.[1] Another would

---

[1] H. F. Redlich, 'Schein and the German Madrigal', *The Listener*, 14 April 1955.

be the several possibilities of performance suggested by Michael Praetorius for his chorale arrangements in the *Musae Sionae* (from 1601)—*cantus-fermus*-wise ('Ist etwa eine Clausul mit dem Texte aus dem *Chorale* genommen und dieselbe *Contrapunctsweise* zum gantzen *Choral* durch und durch geführet'), fugue-wise ('fugeweis *ad aequales*'), motet-wise ('*ad imitationem Orlando di Lasso* auff Muteten Art'), and in the manner of the Italian madrigal ('*ad imitationem Lucae Marentij* und anderer *Italorum* auff Madrigalische Art').[1] No vestige of the *cantus fermus* is to be found in Hassler's *Neüe teütsche gesang*, but it does contain features of the second and third of these styles. The contra- Ex. 5 puntal opening of *Ich scheid von dir mit Leide*, in conjunction with a text less Italianate than some, makes rather a conservative impression, and the relationship of the parts, their mainly stepwise movement, and the relative absence of stress, would not be out of keeping with liturgical music. But the piece sheds some of its contrapuntal qualities, and in the latter sections the technique is often predominantly chordal. The setting of *Dein Äuglein klar*, to take another example, also starts Ex. 6 contrapuntally but, with its stronger rhythmic movement, less liturgically. It generates a feeling of dance as the element of stress asserts itself, and reaches a homophonic conclusion. Ex. 7

*Mein Lieb will mit mir kriegen*, however, contains nothing remotely reminiscent of counterpoint and motet. This is essentially secular music which in its confident tonality, its clear-cut harmonies, its assured cadences, the physical energy implied in its boisterous rhythms, and its exuberant joy in a sensuously exciting volume of sound asserts the claims of new and more worldly forms of experience. So much cannot be said on behalf of Regnart's *Kurtzweilige teutsche Lieder*, significant though they are for the changing relationship of music and poetry after the decay of the *Tenorlied*. But they are not so charged with Renaissance feeling as some of Hassler's pieces—which is a way of saying that in these the union of words and music strikes greater depths and absorbs wider and profounder experience. Renaissance feeling, as here understood, involves not only affirmation of the value of things of this world, but also man's right to enjoy them as an individual, whose experience is justified for its own sake and demands freedom to express itself in its individual way.

The next step, therefore, is to observe how, in conjunction with a further and decisive advance in German poetry, the individual voice, liberating itself from the commitments of part-music, comes to assert

[1] 'Nota Autoris ad Lectorem Musicum', prefacing the Ninth Part of the *Musae Sionae*

its claims to greater freedom in an autonomous melodic line. The transitional figure now of immediate importance from this point of view is Johann Hermann Schein, who, even if he had not been a distinguished composer, would have been remembered not without respect as a poet, and it was the interplay of his musical genius and literary ability that made his contribution in this context so significant.

# PART II

⊰⊱ ⊰⊱ ⊰⊱ ⊰⊱ ⊰⊱ ⊰⊱ ⊰⊱ ⊰⊱ ⊰⊱ ⊰⊱ ⊰⊱ ⊰⊱ ⊰⊱ ⊰⊱

## IV

## The Transition to the Continuo Lied

### JOHANN HERMANN SCHEIN
### POET AND COMPOSER

SCHEIN, who was born in 1586 and died in 1630, spent the most important years of his life as cantor in Leipzig, Bach's most distinguished predecessor in that office. He never visited Italy, but he was very familiar with Italian music, and his friendship with Schütz must have contributed to his interest in it. One of his main contacts with German poetry was his friendship with Fleming, whom he first met as a schoolboy at St. Thomas's. Fleming was under Schein there for five years and his earliest extant verse comprises some Latin distichs on the death of Schein's first wife. The friendship may have deepened Schein's knowledge of poetry. It widened Fleming's interest in music, and this affected his verse. Some of it is very obviously musical, like the dance-rhythm of the poem beginning:

> Laßt uns tanzen,
> Laßt uns springen,

significantly described as 'from the Italian'. So too is *O liebliche Wangen*, written to an Italian melody known only by its title (*O fronte serena*), and the poem *Madrigal*, which looks like a translation from an unidentified Italian original. Musical too are the mellifluous cadences of a stanza like the following:

> Es ist umsonst, das Klagen,
> > Das du um mich,
> > Und ich um dich,
> > Wir umeinander tragen.
> Sie ist umsonst, die harte Pein,
> Mit der wir itzt umfangen sein.

For some little time before Schein was appointed to the cantorship, Italian music had been gaining ground in Leipzig. Scandello, whose *Il primo libro delle Canzone Napoletane* was printed in Nuremberg in 1566 and was the first purely Italian collection of vocal music to be published in Germany, is represented in Ammerbach's *Orgel- und Instrumentaltablatur*; this appeared in Leipzig in 1571 and comprises arrangements of some polyphonic songs already popular there. A second edition was issued in 1583, when the tendency was to drop the older polyphonic music in favour of French chansons and Italian madrigals—and Regnart's *Venus du und dein Kind* was included in a four-part arrangement. Most of the lute versions of vocal music in Rude's *Flores musicae* are based on Italian madrigals, less than a quarter on German music; only Hassler, Lechner, and Haussmann are represented. By about 1580 'Italian madrigals were beginning to penetrate into Leipzig, by about 1600 there was a deluge of them'.[1] Any resistance to this tendency was unimportant compared with the appearance of works like Balthasar Fritsch's *Newe deutsche Gesänge nach art der welschen Madrigalien*, published in Leipzig in 1608, only two years before Schein's first vocal work, *Venus Kräntzlein. Mit allerley lieblichen vnd schönen Blumen gezieret vnd gewunden. Oder newe weltliche Lieder*.

Italian influence is felt more significantly, however, in Schein's *Diletti pastorali*, *Hirtenlust*, a set of continuo madrigals of 1624, of which the following is a characteristic text:

> Die Vöglein singen,
> Die Tierlein springen,
> Die Lüftlein sausen,
> Die Bächlein brausen,
> Die Bäumlein lachen,
> Die Felsen krachen,
> Die Schäflein weiden
> Auf grüner Heiden:
> Wenn Filli kommt gegangen,
> Der Wälder Zier und Kron,
> Ihren liebsten Coridon
> Gar freundlich tut umfangen:
> Die Hirten rufen allzugleich:
> O viva Filli tugendreich.

The pastoral background (influenced by the Italian madrigal), lines ranging between seven and fifteen and of varying length (not less than

---

[1] R. Wustmann, *Musikgeschichte Leipzigs*, Leipzig, 1909, p. 292.

four syllables as a rule or more than nine), the modish insertion of an Italian phrase, and memories of folk-song (*auf grüner Heiden*) are among the characteristic features of this kind of poetry. The springy rhythm has been influenced by dance music, while shorter and longer lines intermingle with advantage to the composer.

Schein's genius had been more impressively evident in the *Fontana d'Israel, Israels Brünnlein Auserlesener Krafft Sprüchlein*, continuo madrigals published the previous year in five or six parts with words mainly from the Book of Psalms, and influenced particularly by Monteverdi. In a piece such as *Wende dich, Herr, und sei mir gnädig* chromaticism, dissonance, and written-in dynamics show Schein emulating the Italian composers. There is some imitation and polyphony in the motet style, but Schein's enthusiasm was for a much more affective kind of music, as in his wonderful setting of *Die mit Tränen säen*. On this account he won high praise from Printz in the *Historische Beschreibung der Edelen Sing- und Kling-Kunst*: 'Er ist aber vornehmlich fürtrefflich gewesen in dem *Stylo Madrigalesco*, in welchem er keinem Italiener vielweniger einem andern etwas nachgeben dörffen.'[1]

The emotional depth of the *Fontana d'Israel* contrasts strikingly with the playful pretence of the *Diletti pastorali*. In the former Schein was expressing profound religious feeling within an established musical tradition, enriched by Italian influence, and his texts carried his spiritual conviction. But in the *Diletti pastorali* he was experimenting with modish poetic tricks. The music may have a dramatic vigour far exceeding the limits of his artificial texts, but his musical intentions were as light-hearted as his verse. Poetry like this had only the flimsiest of roots in Germany, and its growth had been artificially stimulated by musical fashion. Forster, reflecting current interest in Italian composers, had in his fifth book put words to Italian madrigal music, and Schallenberg had translated Italian songs into German. It was not long before Italian madrigals began to be printed in Germany. A volume of Marenzio's madrigals appeared in Nuremberg in 1601, and in the same year Haussmann, who shortly before had published in Leipzig Italian villanellas and other pieces with German words, issued a collection of Vecchi's canzonets with German texts. As with the villanella, the conventions were simple and, with sources like the German translation of Guarini's *Il pastor fido* available, easy to copy. The pictorialism in the texts was welcome to composers who had come to admire this aspect in Monteverdi, and madrigals offered the chance

[1] p. 136.

to experiment with the concertante style pioneered by Monteverdi in his Seventh Book of 1619. Few original German texts were available. Fleming, the most gifted among the early baroque poets, wrote only a single madrigal (possibly at Schein's instigation), though he translated some of *Il pastor fido* and paraphrased part of it as an ode.

Between the *Venus Kräntzlein* and the *Diletti pastorali* Schein published in three instalments a collection of fifty songs under the title *Musica boscareccia, Wald Liederlein* (1621–8), for which again he wrote the words and which, as the sub-title indicates, were by derivation villanellas. In the following example the playful use of mythology in a pastoral setting is little more impressive than in many other texts of the time, though, despite some troublesome elisions, the poem has an easy movement unstrained by too close imitation:

> Mirtillo mein, dein Delia,
> Die dich von Herzen liebet,
> In deine Treu und Gratia
> Sich dir heut ganz ergiebet.
> Die Göttr und Nymphen all zugleich
> Mit dir sich hoch erfreuen,
> Im Wald untr einem grün Gesträuch
> Führn einen lustgen Reihen.
>
> Gott Phoebus selbsten dirigirt,
> Die Musik[1] Euch zu Ehren,
> Pallas das Ballet intonirt,
> Ihr Stimmlein rein läßt hören.
> Die Musen all ihr Instrument
> Darein wohl akkordieren,
> Davon die Bäum an allem End
> Ganz lieblich resonieren.
>
> Pan will auch nicht der letzte sein
> Mit seiner Wald-Schalmeien,
> Mercurius sein Lyr stimmt ein,
> Hilft zieren auch den Reihen.
> Dem Bräutigam und seiner Braut
> Insgsamt sie gratulieren,
> Das Echo aus den Talen laut
> Tut ihnen respondieren.

The dance measure of the words, obviously influenced by rhythms familiar to Schein as a musician, determines the general character of Ex. 8 the setting. By the third bar, however, when the music pauses on the

---

[1] At this time *Musik* was stressed on the first syllable.

first syllable of *Herzen*, the dance-rhythm is significantly checked by the impulse of the music to dwell on a feature of the text that particularly interests it and which lends itself to musical elaboration or interpretation. A feature here is the lengthening of the note-values during the phrase *von Herzen liebet*, as happens again in the case of the minim at *ganz*, and then at the expressive fall to the second syllable of *ergiebet*. Performed instrumentally, the music would adequately convey the aspect belonging to the sphere of dance, but at important points it would miss its intended effect.

Schein's skill in uniting words and music in subtler and more complex ways is illustrated by this example:

> O Sternen-Äugelein!
> O Seiden-Härelein!
> O Rosen-Wängelein!
> Korallen-Lippelein!
> O Perlen-Zähnelein!
> O Honig-Züngelein!
> O Perlemutter-Öhrelein!
> O Elfenbeinen-Hälselein!
> O Pomeranzen-Brüstelein!
> Bisher an euch ist alles fein,
> Ab'r: O du steinern Herzelein,
> Wie daß du tötst das Leben mein!

> O grüne Wälderlein!
> O Myrtensträuchelein!
> O kühle Brünnelein!
> Kristallen Bächelein!
> O grüne Wieselein!
> O schöne Blümelein!
> O Felsenkluft, o Berg und Tal.
> O Echo, treuer Widerschall!
> O Pan, o Schäf'r und Schäferin:
> Seht doch, wie ich so elend bin!
> Der grimmig Tod mich greifet an.
> Ach helfet, wer da helfen kann!

> O wahre Lieb und Treu!
> O falsche Heuchelei!
> O Hoffnung, Sicherheit!
> O Furcht, Schwermütigkeit!
> O süße Lust und Freud!
> O Angst und Herzenleid!
> O Musik, edler Freudenschall!
> O Seufzen, Heulen, Herzensknall!

O Leben, Lieb, o bitter Tod!
Ach wechselt um, es ist die Not!
Wie könntet ihr doch alle sehn
Ein liebend Herz zu Trümmern gehn!

The number of lines in each stanza is within the usual limits of madrigalian poetry, where such variation in the length of lines was normal. The lavish use of diminutives and metaphors, the reference to Pan and Echo, to shepherds and shepherdesses, and the antithetical conceits in the last stanza are all conventional features. The first stanza, describing and reflecting upon the beloved, is the most artificial part of the poem, with its contrived pairing of features and its metaphorical extravagance. In the second, the poet, standing aside from immediate concern with his beloved's physical attractions, contemplates nature as the symbol of certainty and fidelity. The diminutives appear more natural in this context; *O schöne Blümelein* could suggest folk-song associations. In the invocation to nature there is an arranged pairing of aspects as in the preceding verse, but the artifice is less disturbing. The beloved is the theme of the first stanza, nature of the second. In the third, description yields to reflection, and an altered rhyming scheme juxtaposes the fickleness and sorrows of love with the faithfulness of nature. The diminutives vanish, and, forsaking Pan and the shepherds, the poem speaks with a more natural voice.

In the setting features like those which occasionally differentiate *Mirtillo mein* from a dance-song pure and simple are very much more marked. One could be forgiven for not thinking of this as a villanella or a dance at all. The music is not bound to any metrical pattern and creates the impression of flowing naturally from the text. How intimate is the relation of words and music can be appreciated if, in the following analysis, we bear in mind the lifeless text of the religious adaptation attached to Schein's setting in the seventeenth century and which in comparison fits it only in a superficial way:

O mühselige Zeit!
O Unbeständigkeit!
O Widerwärtigkeit!
O täglich neuer Streit!
O Furcht und Herzeleid,
Betrug und Eitelkeit!
O Leben voller Todespein!
O Larvenwerk und falscher Schein!
O Sorg und Müh, o schlimmer Lohn!

Ach wär ich doch einmal davon!
Hat doch sein eigen Not und Plag
Ein jeder, auch der beste Tag!

O wertest Ewigkeit!
O wahre Seligkeit!
O große Herrlichkeit!
O Freud ohn Traurigkeit!
O Fried ohn Sorg und Streit!
O Lieb ohne alles Leid!
O Leben ohne Sterblichkeit!
O Augenlust ohn Eitelkeit!
O Reichtum ohne Flüchtigkeit!
Der Glaub besitzt dich all bereit,
Nur daß so lange wird die Zeit,
Bis auch das Schauen mache Freud!

O Jesu, treuer Hort!
O edle Lebenspfort!
O teures wertes Wort,
Du leuchtest immer fort
Bis zu dem Himmelsport,
Nichts hindert Zeit und Ort!
Ach laß sich meines Lebens Zeit
Durch dich so mit der Ewigkeit
Verbinden, daß ich keine Stund
Vergesse, was dein süßer Mund
Mich lehret, bis dem Jammertal
Nachfolge deiner Freuden Saal.

Without the music the first nine lines of each stanza (of the original text) would appear as an undifferentiated sequence of parallel statements. But the music, uniform in rhythm down to the first syllable of *Perlen-Zähnelein*, has subtle melodic variation. In the top part there is a general pattern determined by the rise after the first quaver of each phrase to the first stressed syllable of every line, but the interval is always different—a semitone in the first line, a fourth in the second, a semitone in the third, and a second in the fourth line. In the poem each verse would seem to rise to a climax at *O Pomeranzen-Brüstelein*, and the equivalent point in the other stanzas, but the music tells a different story. The rise from the first line to the second intensifies the feeling associated with *O Seiden-Härelein*, but thereafter, over a descending bass, the melody falls through a near-sequence at the lines: Ex. 9

O Rosen-Wängelein!
Korallen-Lippelein!

The setting of:

> O Perlen-Zähnelein!
> O Honig-Züngelein!

has a similar character, though these lines begin their fall a second above the earlier ones, emphasized by the longer note-values, as the section drops to its cadence at the lowest note.

In the song (but not in the poem) a climax is reached in the seventh line. For the first time the exclamatory *O* is a note longer than a quaver; it is the highest note so far, approached by a leap of a tenth. At the words:

> O Perlemutter-Öhrelein!
> O Elfenbeinen-Hälselein!
> O Pomeranzen-Brüstelein!

the melody follows an earlier tendency in the descending pattern of the successive *O*'s, but the dotted rhythm, a new feature, introduces a mood of agitation. More important, whereas in the opening section the stress had fallen mainly in the third beat of the bar, now it falls on the second, and this has important implications. In the first four lines the music, rising to the first syllable of the substantive, attaches the poet's feeling to the metaphorical aspect of the lady's features, to her eyes as stars, her hair as silk, her cheeks as roses, and her coral lips. But now the music singles out for attention not so much the pearl, the ivory, or the pomegranate, but ears, neck, and breasts. Added to the effect of the dotted crochet on the first syllable of *Zähnelein* and *Züngelein*, together with the additional stress carried by the longer note, the change is a significant one, shifting the emphasis in the lines now under discussion from the metaphor to the physical reality.

As his own poet, Schein had special advantages, and his poem was no doubt shaped by the music envisaged for it. This is evident particularly in his ability to produce a telling musical effect appropriate to more than the opening stanza. The initial three-quaver figure in the setting of:

> Bisher an euch ist alles fein

reproduces a characteristic feature of the first section, but it also introduces something new. It differs mainly in its rhythmic character, which resembles neither the swaying movement of the opening lines nor the dotted rhythm of the bars immediately preceding it. Hitherto the three-quaver figure has been associated with rhythmic movement, but this ceases as the quavers give way to two crochets and these in turn lengthen to three minims. The music loses all connexion with dance and generates something of the expressive force of Italian monody. What would be read as a line of reflective comment is made by the music into an impassioned outburst, through the effect of the lengthening notes in conjunction with the diatonic rise to the F natural. Despite its individual features, the setting is equally appropriate to:

> Seht doch, wie ich so elend bin!

in the next stanza, and to:

> O Leben, Lieb, o bitter Tod!

in the final stanza. Likewise the discord of a second on the first syllable of *Herzelein* fits the corresponding line of the following verse:

> Der grimmig Tod mich greifet an.

It is not out of keeping with:

> Ach helfet, wer da helfen kann!

and it has a particular contribution to make to:

> Ein liebend Herz zu Trümmern gehn!

This is a lyrical poem, but it dramatizes the lover's situation, and the music makes the climax essentially a dramatic one. This is the effect of the last three bars, where, in a way learnt from the Italians, the double use of the augmented triad screws up the harmony in a passage of dramatic intensity.

Schein's *O Sternen-Äugelein* exploits affective resources much more than the piece by Hassler examined in the previous chapter, and, whereas in some of Hassler's texts in the *Neüe teütsche gesang*, as in the music, there are traditional features, the texts of the *Musica boscareccia* are all extremely up to date, and so is the music, even though some of it is not free from modality. As in Hassler's piece the tune of *O Sternen-Äugelein* is in the top part, but with the important difference that, being not merely the upper note of a series of chords and completing a structure laid by others as equals, it has greater life and freedom of its own. Not dependent on the other parts for its direction, it can react more sensitively to the lyrical flexibility of the text. But the musical structure which allows it this freedom and opportunity is slightly ambiguous, reflecting indecision in Schein's mind between the claims of part-music and solo song.

While he composed two pieces expressly as continuo songs, he refrained from including them in his collected works. One is entitled *Jocus Nuptialis* ('à sola Voce, uff einer Tiorben, etc., zu spielen'), a short dance-song for a wedding, with an opening very similar to *Mirtillo mein*. The other, not included in Prüfer's modern edition, is a tenor song, *Fürwahr er trug unsre Kranckheit*. As to the *Musica boscareccia*, the full sub-title runs: *Auff italian-Villanellische Invention beydes für sich allein mit lebendiger Stim, oder in ein Clavicimbel, Spinet, Tiorba, Lauten etc. Wie auch auff musicalischen Instrumenten anmuthig vnd lieblich zu spielen.* Six alternative possibilities of performance are offered, which for the record it may be useful to have in the original:

Es können diese meine Liedlein füglich musicirt werden:
(1) Alle drey Stimmen, als der Baß und zwene Soprani, in ihrer natürlichen Höhe, entweder für sich allein oder auch in ein Corpus, etc.
(2) Daß man die zweene Soprani oder Discante in Tenoren verwandeln, eine Oktave niedriger, dem Gehör auch nicht unannehmlich seyn.
(3) Daß man Soprano 1 lasse einen Discant bleiben, aus Soprano 2 aber einen Tenor machen.
(4) Daß man die Soprani vivâ voce singen, und den Baß auf einer Trombone, Fagot oder Violin fein still darzu spielen lasse.
(5) Daß man Soprano 1 vivâ voce singen, Soprano 2 aber auf einem Violin oder Flötlein; und den Baß auff jetzt gedachter Instrumenten einem darzu machen lassen.
(6) Kann der Baß, wenn man ein Corpus etc. dabey hat; oder auch wol in mangelung der discantistin, Soprano 2, auff Concertart gantz ausgelassen werden.

Nos. 1–3 are concerned merely with alterations of pitch, and no. 6 has to do with the question of choral performance. Nos. 4 and 5 are the significant ones, because they allow the bass to become a continuo accompaniment. No. 5 is the more important, since it would go a long way towards making these pieces continuo songs for a single voice (with obligato). The bass in any case is figured, as if inviting performance on a harmonic instrument, like lute or keyboard.

A revealing discussion of another item in Schein's collection (*O Berg und Tal ihr Felsen all*) observes that the equality of parts is abandoned and, performed as song for a solo voice, the 'monodic expressive power' of the upper part would be readily appreciated—but that, finding it apparently difficult to maintain this feature throughout, in the second part Schein tends towards a style more in keeping with more traditional part-music.[1] There is some uncertainty even in *O Sternen-*

[1] E. Bücken, *Das deutsche Lied*, Hamburg, 1939, p. 18.

*Äugelein.* The way the three-quaver figure is treated makes one sometimes think of contrapuntal imitation, and, since it occurs quite often in other songs in the *Musica boscareccia*, Schein found it apparently useful for structural purposes. But in this particular piece it is easily absorbed into the melodic line and becomes one of its characteristic features. After all, Schein was primarily a vocal composer, and the *Banchetto musicale*, consisting of pavanes, galliards, and suchlike, was his only purely instrumental work.

The success of the *Musica boscareccia* reveals that the trend of taste was ready to accept the new direction in which it pointed. It provided some of the most popular songs of the period of the Thirty Years War and the history of its various editions reflects the interest awakened. The first edition was published by the composer ('in Verlegung des Autoris'), and in 1627 a second edition was published likewise at Leipzig. A year later there was a reprint in Strassburg and in 1631 a reprint by the original *Selbstverlag*, followed the year after by another printing in Strassburg. In 1634 a further edition, described as Part One, appeared in Dresden. Part Two was almost as successful, several editions being issued in the years 1626–41. Part Three called for rather fewer printings, but there were several both by the *Selbstverlag* and at Dresden. These facts are important also in a literary connexion. This is poetry good enough not to require music to give it melody and rhythm, but it was only in conjunction with music and with its assistance that as yet it could reach more than the narrowest circle of connoisseurs.

Trends noted earlier in the relationship of words and music from vocal polyphony through Regnart and Hassler are seen in Schein in their logical evolution. The growing hegemony of the upper part makes it obvious that with Schein we stand on the threshold of the continuo lied. He is the most significant figure in this connexion, but not the only composer who would have to be discussed in a comprehensive account of the transitional developments.[1] Vetter instances a song in Steuccius's five-part *Newe Schöne Lustige Deudsche Weltliche Lieder* (1602–3) where the upper voice shows an interesting freedom of movement, but it is hardly substantial or significant enough to justify the statement that 'the moment when this song was first sung has historical

---

[1] The evidence recently adduced by Denis Stevens indicating the existence of contemporary arrangements from Renaissance German song-books of songs for solo voice and lute would also have to be mentioned, though, while they helped to prepare the way for solo song, they would only amount to adaptations of part-music. Cf. D. Stevens (ed.), *A History of Song*, London, 1960, pp. 94–95.

significance. It heralded the coming of a new age.'[1] As Vetter also remarks,[2] the smoothness of some of Steuccius's texts calls for comment, rather more than twenty years before Opitz reformed German prosody.

Schein's work has the special feature that, while some of his songs are essentially dance-songs, others (like *O Sternen-Äugelein*) justify reference to arioso song through the extent to which the music follows the inflexion of the words. In *A Plaine and Easie Introduction to Practicall Musicke* Morley formulated the principle here referred to in a famous passage:

> We must also have a care so to applie the notes to the wordes as in singing there be no barbarisme committed; that is, that cause no syllable that is by nature short to be expressed by many notes, or one long note, nor so long a syllable to be expressed with a short note.

From Dowland through the Cavalier composers to Purcell England has many striking examples of arioso, declamatory song which, standing in a line of development from Italian monody, proved wonderfully apt for the often quite dramatic expression of nuances of feeling, and in which, in Byrd's phrase about his *Psalmes, Sonets, and Songs* of 1611, music could be 'framed to the life of the words'. In Germany, however, such music was never to win sustained approval in the baroque lied, rather in the same way that madrigal verse was never able to establish itself in Germany, efforts to win favour for it always having an element of special pleading.

The history of the baroque lied illustrates at many different points the reluctance to advance on the lines of arioso song, to 'shape Notes to the Words and Sense'. The reasons include the effects of the religious struggle in a country where the situation was complicated by the coexistence of adjacent courts of rival faiths—so that in the Protestant areas, where the lied mainly flourished, there was resistance to cultural forces with transalpine connexions, while the Protestant chorale, a weapon in the religious struggle, often coloured the baroque lied. Bukofzer touches on this aspect when in a wider context he says that, 'while the Catholic composers adopted the Italian style without essential changes, the Protestant composers were faced with the task of bringing their precious heritage, the chorale, in harmony with the concertato style. The result of this fusion was the most original German contribution to the history of baroque music.'[3] But Schein's handling

---

[1] W. Vetter, 'Wort und Weise im deutschen Kunstlied', *Zeitschrift für Musikwissenschaft*, x.          [2] *Das frühdeutsche Lied*, Münster, 1928, p. 53.
[3] *Music in the Baroque Era*, New York, 1947, p. 78.

of the chorale had features of its own, and these are related to his individual characteristics as a song composer. 'Not content with the presentation of the chorale', Bukofzer remarks about his *Opella nova*, 'Schein strove at the same time for a highly subjective interpretation. In his desire to interpret the affection of the words he distorted the chorale tunes, broke them up into fragments, vivified the rhythm, and infused them with extraneous chromaticism or exuberant *gorgia*.'[1]

The *Musica boscareccia*, in short, was an 'attempt in a new style . . . which let the form develop quite freely, guided by the text and the individual word'.[2] This is an opposite tendency to Bach's, of whom on the contrary it would often be true to say that he sees his texts as 'symbols of meaning not primarily of a linguistic nature, but rather as points of reference to the meaning he perceives beyond the mere words'.[3] Consequently Bach was often well served by poetically indifferent texts, and also his vocal music exhibits characteristics leading to its being sometimes described as instrumental—a feature that has been expressed by saying that with Bach 'in serving language music itself becomes language'.[4] The melody of *O Sternen-Äugelein* is primarily in terms of the voice, flowing from the very essence of the words, with an interest in the quality of the poetry, and it is no coincidence that the most successful number of the *Musica boscareccia* is one in which the poet's art is at its most subtle, delicate, and refined.

[1] Ibid., p. 85.
[2] H. Kretzschmar, *Geschichte des neuen deutschen Liedes*, Leipzig, 1911, p. 12.
[3] Thr. Georgiades, *Musik und Sprache. Das Wesen der abendländischen Musik dargestellt an der Vertonung der Messe*, Berlin–Göttingen–Heidelberg, 1954, pp. 75–76.
[4] H. H. Eggebrecht, 'Über Bachs geschichtlichen Ort', *Deutsche Vierteljahrschrift für Literaturwissenschaft und Geistesgeschichte*, xxxi, 1957, p. 543. Cf. also R. Bullivant, 'Word-Painting and Chromaticism in the Music of J. S. Bach', *Music Review*, xx, 1959, p. 215: 'In fact, it would seem that words, for Bach, act in the vast majority of cases as a trigger which, given the right musical circumstances, sets off, so to speak, an excursus into chromaticism which would anyway be appropriate from a purely musical point of view.'

# V

## The Creation of the Continuo Lied

### MARTIN OPITZ AND JOHANN NAUWACH

IT may have been fortuitous that Opitz's poetry came into Nauwach's hands, and only the mood of the moment that led him to set particular texts in a particular way. The fact is, however, that the creation of the continuo lied in the strict sense of the term was the work of a young and virtually unknown composer who chose, or was persuaded, to set to music verse by the first writer ambitious, talented, and authoritative enough for it to have been claimed on his behalf that he had fashioned a new kind of poetry. In the hands of Regnart and Schein German poetry had under the guidance of music become more elegant, tidier, and more refined. Some of their verse Opitz could not but have approved of, though the purism of his prohibition of elision and of his insistence on a strictly observed pattern of regularly alternating stress set standards they could not always satisfy.

The features of Opitz's poetry that led to its being thought of as new were, in general, those qualities—technical rather than inspirational—through which it asserted its claim to be regarded as worthy in its own right. Nevertheless, he was set to music more often and in more different ways than probably any other poet of the time, a fact due more to his prestige than to anything else. His composers include minor figures like Caspar Kittel, whose *Arien und Kantaten* appeared at Dresden in 1648, Johann Weichmann, who published his *Sorgenlägerin* at Königsberg in the same year, and Erasmus Kindermann, composer of the *Optianischer Orpheus* six years earlier—men whose work with good reason is never heard on the concert platform and who survive only in the corners of musical histories. Others, like Dedekind (*Älbianische Musenlust*, 1657), are among the minor masters of the period, while Albert and Adam Krieger, who also used texts by Opitz, are composers of significance. So also was Hammerschmidt, whose *Weltliche Oden* (from 1642) includes a setting of Opitz's *Wohl dem, der weit von hohen Dingen* that Zesen in his novel *Die Adriatische Rosenmund* (1645) assumed to be widely known, because it must have been this setting that he had in mind when he described his *Lohb-lihd auff drei schöne Jungfrauen zu Uträcht* as going to the tune of Opitz's poem. Hammerschmidt also used religious verse by Opitz in the second part of his *Geistliche Dialoge* ('darinnen Herr Opitzens Hohes Lied Salomis'). Gräfe used a poem by Opitz in his *Sammlung verschiedener auserlesener Oden* as late as 1737. More curiously even, Opitz figures among the texts included in the *Lieder der Teutschen*, dating from the second half of the eighteenth century, a product of the very unbaroque Berlin School.

Opitz's interest in music was not very profound, though as a cultured person he had some knowledge of it, and was not indifferent to its advantages in certain circumstances for poetry. He wrote a number of poems to existing tunes, and this encouraged the metrical regularity of his verse. He may have begun to observe the principle of metre based on a strict pattern of stress as early as 1619,[1] which would be significant, since in that year he went to Heidelberg, where he wrote words to some popular songs (like the *Hirtenlied* to the tune of *Auprès du bord de la Seine*). His *Episteln der Sonntage und fürnehmsten Feste des gantzen Jahres* (1624) were strophic poems to Goudimel's Psalm melodies. But, whatever the virtues of their poetry, in contrast to Regnart and Schein it was Opitz's conscious aim—and the respect he earned in his time stemmed from acknowledgement of his leadership in this respect—to raise poetry to a level at which it would be self-justified by its quality and dignity. His Latin poetry and his alexandrine verse, which in intention least require or by their nature least invite musical assistance, are the extreme examples of this desire. The rules he laid down in his *Buch von der deutschen Poeterey* (1624) are not easily acquitted of the charge of pedantry, but a mitigating factor is Opitz's wider and entirely praiseworthy intention. According to this, poetry was to be a task worthy of a scholar and a gentleman, and it was due to Opitz that accomplishment in this sphere came to be regarded as a feature by which educated middle-class people could earn for themselves a distinction corresponding in its own way to that which was the right of the aristocracy by birth. In the *Fruchtbringende Gesellschaft* nobility was one qualification for membership; cultivated attainments like the writing of poetry constituted another. Poetry with such pretensions could not be satisfied with merely providing words for a composer's convenience, or with supposing that it needed to be improved with the help of a rival craft.

It is true that in his theory Opitz found a place for poetry to be

[1] M. Szyrocki, *Martin Opitz*, Berlin, 1956, pp. 28–29.

sung, but the terms in which he speaks about 'lyrics or poems that particularly lend themselves to musical setting' suggest that he did not regard such poems as of the highest dignity. For, with a reference to Horace, he goes on to describe them as dealing 'with the things that can be contained in a short poem: love, dances, banquets, fine people, gardens, vineyards, the praise of moderation, the unimportance of death, &c., but especially exhortations to jollity'.[1] Probably his attitude was coloured by his conception of the role of music in the classical ode. The emphasis is thus on the lighter and often more trivial topics.

A model illustration of Opitz's technical principles is provided by the following well-known example:

> Ach Liebste laß uns eilen,
> Wir haben Zeit:
> Es schadet das Verweilen
> Uns beiderseit.
>
> Der edlen Schönheit Gaben
> Fliehn Fuß für Fuß,
> Daß alles was wir haben
> Verschwinden muß.
>
> Der Wangen Zier verbleichet,
> Das Haar wird greis,
> Der Augen Feuer weichet,
> Die Brunst wird Eis.
>
> Das Mündlein von Korallen
> Wird ungestalt,
> Die Hand als Schnee verfallen,
> Und du wirst alt.
>
> Drum laß uns jetzt genießen
> Der Jugend Frucht,
> Eh als wir folgen müssen
> Der Jahre Flucht.
>
> Wo du dich selber liebest,
> So liebe mich,
> Gib mir, daß, wann du giebest,
> Verlier auch ich.

Obviously the poem does not spring from any depth of feeling, and its images and metaphors, and the theme itself, are conventional. The conceits in the last verse appear rather as a clever conclusion to a logical argument, and it would be foolish to suppose that the poem

[1] *Das Buch von der deutschen Poeterey*, ed. W. Braune, Tübingen, 1954, p. 22.

addresses any particular woman, or that it was written because the poet was in love. Opitz himself would have assented to comments of this kind, and, questioned about the form of his poem, he would most likely have spoken mainly of the obvious structural features, the neatness of the stanzas, the careful use of iambics, and all that contributes to its effect as polished and cultured verse. Nevertheless, its metrical uniformity is not entirely exclusive of rhythmic interest. The fourth line of the first verse, for example, has individual qualities that make it pleasingly different from the second line, and the same applies to the corresponding lines of the next stanza. The alternation of longer and shorter lines produces the effect of a series of cadences. The poem is attractive to read if only because it flows melodiously. But any musical qualities that this or any other poem by Opitz may have are the result of his efforts to make his poetry good enough to be judged on its own merits. Paradoxically, however, it has features that would claim attention, if it were being analysed as a poem written for music. It happens to accord with the practice of Elizabethan lyrical poets who tended to 'regard the line as the rhythmical unit',[1] because it could save the composer certain difficulties by bringing it about that the rhyme at the end would conveniently fall on a cadence. Also, it lacks the 'complex association of ideas, subtle play of wit', that music cannot hope to copy, it has the 'simple emotions . . . atmospheres and moods with a broad sweep',[2] that suit the purposes of the composer, and it is without 'bold, intense or closely-wrought images' inappropriate to verse written for musical setting, 'since they tend to destroy the balance between the word-pattern and the melodic line'.[3] But the reasons for this go no deeper than Opitz's urbane elegance, his restrained expression of sentiment, and avoidance of complications of feeling beyond conventional limits.

Often, it is true, in Opitz's verse metre tends to stifle rhythm, and this was markedly the case in a lot of verse written under his influence. Even at its best his poetry could offer music nothing comparable to the flexible rhythms of Dowland's texts, which enable the poet 'to modulate through a series of changing rhythms' the diminishing lines sustained 'by the heightening qualities of single words'.[4] The reference here is to the English school of lutenist song writers, most of whose important songs had appeared by 1612. The date, some twelve

[1] B. Pattison, *Music and Poetry in the English Renaissance*, London, 1948, pp. 146, 147.
[2] Ibid., p. 142.
[3] C. Day Lewis, *The Poetic Image*, London, 1947, p. 49.
[4] M. Evans, *English Poetry in the Sixteenth Century*, London, 1955, p. 115.

years before Opitz's *Buch von der deutschen Poeterey*, deserves emphasis as a comment by implication on the relative backwardness, despite the progress made, of German language, poetry, and prosody. This may be one reason why Dowland's influence on German song was negligible, though it was nowhere very great. But he did pay two visits to Germany, first at the invitation of Duke Heinrich Julius von Braunschweig in 1595, and the second time in 1622–3. It is true that by the first, and more important, of these visits he had only as yet published his five Psalm settings (in Thomas East's *The Whole Book of Psalms*), but works of his were published in Heidelberg, Cologne, Frankfurt, Nuremberg, and Augsburg between 1600 and 1621, and Lechner and Schop made instrumental arrangements of *Flow my Tears*. The tune of Dowland's that reappears most frequently in Germany is the four-part galliard *Can she excuse my wrongs with virtue's cloak?* One piece in Voigtländer's *Allerhand Oden vnd Lieder* (1652) is derived from it, the melody of Rist's poem *Daphnis Lobgedicht auff eine Tugendreiche Schäfferin* (in *Galathee*, 1642) uses it, so too does one of Krieger's *Arien*. But the tendency in these imitations is for the subtler rhythmic interest to get lost.

The pioneering, but not the most celebrated, figure among those who set Opitz's poetry to music was Johann Nauwach, who, as the servant of a prince, led in this respect a representative type of baroque musical existence. This had its advantages and disadvantages. It subjected a composer to authority that could be irksome, but a composer in this position shared some of the reflected glory of princely magnificence, enjoyed security, and, since his work was indispensable at court, usually had no great difficulty in getting it performed. At the courts it was possible to 'try out new forms without being bothered too much by tradition', to 'experiment and be sure of finding an understanding audience for music that might cause surprise by its novelty'.[1] Johann Beer, the novelist, who abandoned a middle-class career after studying theology in Leipzig, and joined the musical establishment of the Duke of Sachsen-Weissenfels, decided that 'a musician at court has the best life of all'.[2] The typical baroque poet in Germany wrote in his spare time and earned his living in some administrative post in connexion with a court or some high dignitary, as with Opitz and Gryphius, or, like Rist, in an independent profession. Music,

---

[1] From the article on 'Baroque' in Blume (ed.), *Die Musik in Geschichte und Gegenwart*, Cassel and Basel, 1949 ff.

[2] Quoted by R. Alewyn in his postscript to the Rowohlt edition of Beer's *Das Narrenspiel* and *Jucundi Jucundissimi Wunderliche Lebensbeschreibung*.

however, though not necessarily merely composition, could be a whole-time occupation, and this was the case with Nauwach. He was born in Brandenburg about 1597, the year of Opitz's birth. Having an excellent voice, he was employed as a boy at the Saxon court in 1607, and five years later Elector Johann Georg I, who had close personal ties with Duke Emanuel of Savoy, sent him to study music in Turin, but he successfully sought permission to move to Florence. There he devoted himself largely to the study of the lute and became a virtuoso. Little is known about his life after he was recalled in 1618. Fleming mentions him as still alive in the poem *An Herrn Johan Klipstein*:

> . . . Wenn Schützens Lieder klingen,
> so wächst des Sachsen Lust. Wenn Nauwach das Pandor
> läßt hören und mit ihm den künstlichen Tenor,
> da wacht mein Opitz auf, daß er des Künstlers Stimmen,
> so hoch, wo über uns der Leier Sternen klimmen,
> durch seinen ersten Preis die deutschen Vers empört,
> weil immer eine Kunst die ander' hebt und ehrt.

In Lappenberg's edition no date is attached to this poem, but none of the dated poems in the *Poetische Wälder* are before 1630, and the context of this one in Lappenberg's mainly chronological arrangement would place it about 1630 or 1631. There has been the suggestion that Nauwach died of the plague that struck Dresden in 1630. This was nine years before Opitz died of that disease, thirteen years after his first discussion in the *Aristarchus sive de contemptu Linguae Teutonicae* of the way to revive and reform German poetry, and six years after his most important contribution to this end in the *Buch von der deutschen Poeterey*.

When Nauwach returned to Germany, Opitz was already well known through the *Aristarchus*, and ten years later, in 1628, he was ennobled, largely through the influence of Graf Hannibal von Dohna, whose secretary he became (though Opitz was a Protestant and the count an enemy of his faith) and to whom he dedicated the *Lob des Kriegsgottes* (1628). His most successful poetry, *Trost Gedichte in Widerwertigkeit des Krieges* (1633), was dedicated to a subsequent Protestant patron, Duke Ulderich of Holstein, son of the King of Denmark, 'patriae meae libertatisque tutela'. Nauwach seems to have had personal contact with Opitz, perhaps through Schütz, and to have had access to some of his poems before they were published in the *Oden* in 1628, the year after he used some of them in his *Teutsche*

*Villanellen.* About half the texts are known to be by Opitz. Others may be too. They are of poorer quality than those of which his authorship is certain, which might suggest that he decided not to include them in his published work. He expressed his gratitude to Nauwach for having through his music given his poetry its 'soul'—though in an age accustomed to formal flattery the statement need not be taken at its face value:

> Daß du mein Kinderspiel mit solchem Eifer hebst,
> Und durch dein Singen ihm erst seine Seele giebst.

Nauwach's earlier work, *Libro primo di Aire passegiate à una voce per cantar e sonar nel chitarrone*, is a pastiche collection of pieces with Italian texts demonstrating the fashionable Italian art of embellishment and copying its more obvious features, possibly to show his patron that he had not been idle. In 1627, adopting quite a different style, Nauwach published the first part of his *Teutsche Villanellen*, though nothing more appeared. Despite the title, some of these pieces have at most only a tenuous connexion with the villanella. Of the nineteen numbers, eight are continuo songs, seven are in two parts, and four in three. The range of the music from rather archaically cast part-music to solo song probably reflects the uncertainty of a young composer open to new ideas in a transitional situation. It is only the continuo lieder that made the collection historically significant, and these are very unequal. Some merely rely on a dance-tune that could exist equally well without a text and would be just as effective on instruments. The result, as so often in the less distinguished type of baroque dance-song, can be to distort the text by stressing the wrong Ex. 10 syllable or unimportant words, as in the case of a galliard included in the *Teutsche Villanellen*.

*Ach Liebste laß uns eilen*, however, is an achievement of quite a different order, and again, as with Schein's song analysed in the previous chapter, it can hardly be entirely fortuitous that the most impressive song in the collection is a setting of the most distinguished text. But the regular iambic beat of Opitz's poem, its characteristic feature from a technical point of view, could have become wearisome if allowed too consistently to determine the metre of the music; at the time of Gluck, speaking in his novel *Hildegard von Hohenthal* about music in a sense hostile to the baroque, Heinse was to go so far as to say: 'In operas written in iambics the composer writing for the voice cannot use the rich resources at his disposal and has to work with disgustingly poor material.'[1] Nauwach handles his metre with care and tact. He transforms the opening phrase into a dactyl, and other phrases too acquire a dactylic character—in the fourth bar, for instance, and the third bar from the end. The result is an attractive interplay between the iambic discipline of the text and the greater flexibility of the music. Some credit for this is nevertheless due also to Opitz's poem which, despite its doctrinaire metrical intentions, has sufficient rhythmic flexibility to make such liberties possible without their becoming incongruous.

Music had, if only superficially, influenced the order and pattern of Opitz's poem, and musical experience of a different kind, Italian Ex. 11 monody, enriches Nauwach's setting of it. A slow dance, it nevertheless has features justifying a reference to speech rhythms, like the figure of three quavers in the third and tenth bars, and the opening of the second section. A point to notice is how, over a falling bass, the music finds descending points of rest, marked also by an extra degree of stress on longer notes. Not everybody might be willing to accept the view that the effect is to hint at the suggestion of tolling the knell of passing time. It is certainly a feature of considerable rhythmic interest in its way, and it is helped by the drooping cadences in the text—a musical element in the poem, one might say, and as such an involuntary by-product of the general intention to write poetry able itself to supply all its needs. The music can be effective in these ways only because, as a continuo lied, its melodic line has the necessary independence. Even the better examples of part-music in the *Teutsche Villanellen*, with their more square-cut symmetry, are less expressive than the solo songs. In this piece the bass, moreover, is no longer just a structural element, or merely the root of a series of chords with the tune at the top. Freed from counterpart and imitation, which to some extent still affect the bass of Schein's *O Sternen-Äugelein*, it lends expressive harmonic support to the melody without constraining it, as when it dictates the simple but touching modulation to C major at the reference to *Gaben*. It has, in short, life and purpose, a personality of its own.

The bass of a continuo lied is in essence only a harmonic foundation and, at its simplest, may have no particular distinctive features. It includes, however, the realization and, in skilful hands, this can be subtle and elaborate. Often in a continuo lied the relation of a perceptively realized bass to the upper part will acquire an element of

[1] Insel-Verlag edition of Heinse's *Sämtliche Werke*, v, Leipzig, 1903, p. 360.

drama, as there tends to be between the parts of the better baroque
trio sonatas. To speak of drama in baroque music is immediately to
think of opera, though this may seem out of place regarding so simple
and short a song as Nauwach's *Ach Liebste laß uns eilen.* Circumstances,
however, demand it. Schütz's opera *Dafne* (using Opitz's translation
of a text by Rinuccini) was performed at the celebrations of the
engagement of Landgraf Georg II of Hesse and Sophie Eleonore,
daughter of the reigning Elector of Saxony, Johann Georg I. It was
to this bridal pair that Nauwach dedicated his *Teutsche Villanellen* and
on the same occasion probably presented it, or had it presented, to
them.

Although by a significant coincidence the German continuo lied and
German opera thus began their existence together, one of the factors
most favourable to the growth of the one was to prove most damaging
for the other. The problem here touched upon, serious in its consequences for the further harmonious co-operation of music and
poetry in song, was posed by the very creation of the continuo lied.
What was involved was a question of balance between two arts,
neither of which could ideally fulfil its role in the partnership without limiting its claims, the inherent problem of tension between the
restraints of small-scale strophic poetry and the affective ambitions
of baroque composers anxious that music should not be denied the
fuller use of its expressive resources.

What would Schütz, whose early madrigal music, for example, so
abounds in instances of the affective and dramatic representation of
the words, have made of *Ach Liebste laß uns eilen*? The question is
tantalizing, because he did actually put it to music, but his setting,
known of from early library lists, has disappeared. We still have his
madrigal settings of a few poems by Opitz. *Itzt blicken durch des
Himmels Saal*, in five parts with two violins and bass, tells the story
of a love-lorn student. The higher voices describe the starlit sky, while
the tenor sings his lament in an extremely affective style. The sobbing
figure at *schlafen*, and the semi-quaver figure at the reference to the
play of fish in water, are typical touches of word-painting. The movement of the parts also helps expressively to interpret the text, as when
the bass sings of peace undisturbed by passion. But it is significant
that Schütz found that his intention to write music in this style was
inhibited by the nature of the text. Thus in a letter of 11 December
1653 to Caspar Ziegler, who in that year published a treatise to encourage the writing of madrigal verse, Schütz said that this work had

cost him a lot of trouble 'before I could get it into the form of Italian music'.

Opitz's view of poetry intended for music as entertaining rather than profound corresponds to a common attitude among baroque composers to small-scale strophic songs. Many cultivated it, but often spoke of it no more than condescendingly, and in sophisticated musical circles in seventeenth-century Germany its standing was lower than in Elizabethan England. The multitude of puny dynastic establishments in Germany were dominated by a narrowly courtly culture, and middle-class life, largely an appendage of the courts, had slender foundations. The popular tended to be regarded as banal, even vulgar, the alternative was artifice and sophistication. Christoph Werner, in the preface to his *Musikalische Arien*, published at Königsberg in 1649, was so bold as to say, with some exaggeration no doubt, that 'vocal compositions without figures are despised'. He and many other composers, who could be quoted to provide similar opinions, are unimportant figures, but of greater weight is the opinion of another Königsberg composer, Heinrich Albert, the first baroque master of the lied. He too shows a rather superior attitude towards strophic song despite its growing popularity, or perhaps because of it, and this only a decade or so after Nauwach had created the new type of song.

# VI

## Friendship, Poetry, and Song, and the Establishment of the Continuo Lied

### THE KÖNIGSBERG POETS AND HEINRICH ALBERT

IT was the songs of Heinrich Albert, who wrote poetry in addition to composing music, that really established the continuo lied. He was extremely prolific, but one does not have to pick and choose particularly carefully to find very many excellent examples. They were addressed in the first instance to a circle of friends and beyond that to a limited, local public. They became widely popular and served to arouse more general interest in the new form pioneered by Nauwach. His songs had been written without any particular audience in mind, whereas for Albert and his friends song was part of normal social activity, joining forces with poetry to provide contributions for birthdays, weddings, and funerals, and to enrich many an evening of informal jollification. Albert, who was thus in a better position to create a public for the continuo lied, had also the advantage of not only being himself a poet, but of having intimate contact with an active and closely knit group of poets, and it was never more true in baroque Germany than at this stage that 'the first condition of a fruitful growth of song was a corresponding basis in poetry'.[1]

Albert's background was that of the new middle-class bureaucracy. His grandfather had been an official in the Thuringian town of Gera, his father occupied an administrative job in Schleiz, not far away, and his mother was the daughter of a mayor of Gera. His elder brother reached quite an exalted position in the little state, and his sisters married influential merchants in the region. He was born in 1604 and in 1619 went to the grammar school at Gera. Three years later, instead of going to the university, he began to study composition under Schütz— his cousin incidentally, not his uncle, as is still sometimes imagined.[2] In the foreword to the sixth part of his *Arien*, however, Albert remarks

---

[1] E. Schmitz, *Geschichte der weltlichen Solokantate*, Leipzig, 1914, p. 220.
[2] The misunderstanding occurs through interpreting *Oheim* in its strictly modern sense.

that he was not trained from youth in the art of music, 'nor did I have any idea of making it my profession', and in 1623 he was sent to study law at Leipzig. Three years later he transferred to Königsberg University, but a year afterwards he abandoned his studies to join a Dutch diplomatic mission, set off with it to Warsaw, was arrested and interned. He returned to Königsberg in 1628, began, in accordance with his parents' wishes as to his future career, to study military science, but soon took the post of organist at Königsberg Cathedral.

He was an admirer of Opitz, so too were all his poet-friends. When Opitz visited Königsberg in 1638, Albert composed a cantata in his honour and later, when Opitz had published his Psalm texts to Goudimel's melodies, he honoured him not only by setting one of these texts, but also by incorporating a slightly modified version of its tune. The poet with whom Albert was most intimate was Simon Dach, who provided about half the texts of the *Arien* and who wrote a deeply felt poem at his death:

> Die Freundschaft muß uns unterhalten,
> Der Mensch ist ein gesellisch Tier,
> Wenn die beginnet zu erkalten
> Was nützt uns lange sein allhier.

Dach also wrote the libretti of Albert's two operas. *Cleomides* was in honour of the visit of King Wladislaw IV of Poland to Königsberg; the music is lost except for two numbers included in the *Arien*. Nothing remains of the music of the other, *Prussiarchus*, celebrating the centenary of Königsberg University. Dach, who evidently felt that Albert's settings had added lustre to his verse:

> Mein Arbeit zog durch deine Weisen
> In Wahrheit neue Kleider an,

was the best of the Königsberg poets, who included Robert Roberthin, to whom Dach wrote a touching poem about friendship (*Danckbarliche Auffrichtigkeit an Herrn Robert Roberthinen*). Another was Christoph Kaldenbach, who was also a composer, and in a volume of songs, *Deutsche Sappho* (1651), figures in both capacities, and also as a collector of other people's songs (including Albert's). The fame of these writers in the seventeenth century was promoted by the popularity of Albert's settings of their verse. As a group of friends they regularly participated in social activities, when poetry and music served to celebrate happy occasions or convey sympathy in times of sorrow. Albert also was connected with the so-called *Kürbs-Hütte*, which had the special function of providing poetry and music for funerals. Its outcome was the *Musicalische Kürbs-Hütte*, for which Albert also provided the texts. Dach's poem *Klage um den endlichen Untergang und ruinierung der Kürbs-Hütte und Gärtchens* is about the demise of this group.

Albert died in 1651, a much loved figure in and around Königsberg, and the students of the university publicly demonstrated their affection. He also wrote motets, hymns, and operas, but his fame rests on the *Arien*. He took quite a modest view of these, however, and in the foreword to the first part (1638) he begged people 'not to imagine that these melodies are intended to show any great skill, for this would do me an injustice. . . . I composed these songs for the sake of the texts, which came into my hands, which I liked, and which for the most part I was asked to put to music by good friends of mine.' Also, slightly apologetically, he wrote: 'If you are surprised that I have included religious and secular songs in one book, remember how it is in your own life. Often you spend time in the morning in worship, but at noon you amuse yourself in the garden or some other pleasant place, and pass the evening in good company, perhaps with your lady love.' In the second part, which appeared in 1640 and was dedicated to Schütz, he was still concerned about possible misunderstandings about the unpretentious nature of the songs, composed when 'the authors of the texts and myself sometimes met to make music merely for our own pleasure'. The third part was published in the same year, part four in 1641. This was expected to be the last, and so he indexed it. The fifth part includes the important reference to songs in it 'of rather special quality' (*besonders feine Lieder*). Ideally, he says, 'every line should have had its own setting', but considerations of cost had deterred him. Part six ('perhaps the last', he thought) appeared in 1645, and it too has an index. In the seventh part Albert seizes the chance to complain about illicit printings which, reflecting the growing popularity of the *Arien*, continued to appear despite official prohibitions in various areas. This is repeated at greater length and with stronger feeling in the eighth part (1650), this time with special reference to a pirated edition entitled *Poetisch Musikalische Lust Wäldlein*. This was of particular moment, because, despite errors and deviations, it threatened to supersede the authentic editions. Albert evidently objected not only to the music but also to the words being tampered with. A ninth part, probably a collection of scattered pieces put together by someone else in the meantime, was announced at the Leipzig Fair of 1676, but no copy survives, if it ever actually appeared.

Albert's mention of the songs 'of rather special quality', which he would have liked to set more ambitiously, is a reference to through-composition. But he did not write simpler strophic songs under protest or pressure, even though he wanted to be sure that people did not think that they displayed his full technical resources. In any case, the poetry provided by his friends did not really call for any other treatment. As they were not writing for public occasions, or for reasons of literary prestige, their verse, always strophic, was relatively simple and unadorned. Albert's attitude was a little contradictory. Clearly he sometimes felt restricted by the strophic continuo lied—but, to encourage correct performance, he took the trouble to introduce the second part with a set of instructions about performance from a figured bass. And the large number of his songs in a simple style testifies to considerable interest on his part.

His thoughts about the advantages of through-composition must have been influenced by what he knew about Italian music, and no doubt he heard a lot about this from Schütz. In the context in which he mentions the *besonders feine Lieder*, he speaks about the 'symphonies and choruses' demanded by more elaborate forms of music, probably a reference to Italian opera and cantata. But one has to be cautious in generalizing about those items in the *Arien* that are more than continuo lieder. Even when he rewrote pieces originally intended for solo voices in parts, the influence was sometimes that of the older motet tradition. Eccard's *Preußische Festlieder*, written at Königsberg some thirty years before, were still remembered, when Albert was beginning his musical career in the town, and were respected as an important manifestation of the polyphonic tradition. At a slightly earlier date vocal polyphony had been intensively cultivated by Duke Albrecht (who had connexions with Senfl) in the service of the Reformation.

An example of the simplest kind of continuo lied is Albert's setting of the following text:

Phyllis, die mich vormals liebet,
Der ich auch mein Herz bedacht,
Hat mich jetzund so betrübet,
Daß ich keiner Freuden acht;
Soll ich sie nicht wiedersehen,
So ist es um mich geschehen.

Phyllis bleibet mir im Herzen,
Und ihr süßer Nam hat mir
Oft erreget solche Schmerzen,
Daß ich mich darin verlier,
Soll ich sie nicht wiedersehen,
So ist es um mich geschehen.

Dennoch hoff ich bald zu kommen
An sie, die mich vormals liebt,
Sie ist's, die mein Herz genommen,
Sie ist's, die mir's wiedergibt,
Und bei ihrer Augen Schein
Werd ich erst erquicket sein.

The poem, which strictly observes Opitz's rules, has few ornamental features, apart from the sophistication of a passing antithesis in the last verse, and a familiar metaphor in the penultimate line. The refrain in the first two stanzas, the way each stanza ends with a cadential effect of a rhyming couplet, and the lilt of the four-stressed iambic lines would make it pretty certain that it was written for music, and its obvious simplicity makes it a suitable text for an informal dance-song. It was, in fact, probably written to an existing French tune; Ex. 12 Albert heads it *aria gallica*, though he may have adapted the melody slightly to fit the words.

Even simpler is the celebrated *Anke von Tharaw*, one of a number of pieces described as *Aria incerti Autoris*. The tune is therefore not Albert's invention, and its origins have been traced back to the late sixteenth century. The instrumental part, a simple fiddle accompaniment to a popular dance, and the Low German dialect, add to the popular flavour.

The first part of the *Arien* contains a setting of Roberthin's 'Conversation of a Young Lady and a Withered Rose Tree', beginning:

| | |
|---|---|
| *Jungfrau.* | Du vormals grüner Stock |
| | Wie stehst du jetzt so wüste? |
| *Rosenstock.* | Gedachtest du denn nicht, |
| | Daß ich auch dorren müßte? |
| *Jungfrau.* | Wo ist die schöne Pracht |
| | Der Rosen hingekommen? |
| *Rosenstock.* | Ein freche Räuberhand |
| | Hat sie mir weggenommen. |

Up to a point a dialogue like this could have dramatic possibilities for a composer with an inclination towards cantata. Albert, however, has no choice but to make it a strophic song, because attempts at expressive elaboration would have been resisted by such a large number of short and identical stanzas. Pieces in the same vein include Dach's *Der Mensch hat nichts so eigen* and a charming setting of Roberthin's Ex. 13 *Mein liebstes Seelchen laßt uns leben.*

A modern transcription of this song would have to bar it in triple time, which could make it look as if Albert sometimes disregarded the natural stress of the words. At the beginning of the second line the accent would fall on the unaccented part of the iambic foot, on *so*, and in the fourth line too. But later in the same line the stress that the music would place on *das* fits nicely the way the phrase could be read in its context. Albert, however, in accordance with the usual practice of the time, uses vertical lines down the stave, not to separate bar from bar as in modern convention, but to divide the song up for the guidance of the performer. His songs combine in an interesting and subtle way the principle of stressed music with memories of the older mensural tradition. Also, since the songs were composed for a group of friends who understood each other's habits, a good deal could be taken for granted. There is clear evidence in Albert's songs about this, though suggestions as to how they should be barred to accord more with modern convention are often open to argument.

Though the simpler kind of strophic lied could thus have greater rhythmic flexibility than might superficially appear, Albert did not always find this sufficient for his purposes, and, freeing himself from the form of the lied altogether, he wrote some undisguised cantatas. Between the two extremes comes a piece like *O der rauhen Grausamkeit!* in which the urge towards cantata is so strong as to come near to undermining the form of the strophic lied:

> O der rauhen Grausamkeit!
> Die nur Seufzen jederzeit
> Mit viel Seufzen häuft,
> O des Lebens ohne Leben,
> Das zum Tode läuft,
> Das in Zittern stets muß schweben!
> Trübsal, Kummer, Herzensglut,
> Solche Liebe geben tut.
>
> Ist es denn der Sternen Kraft,
> Daß wir werden hingerafft
> In die Dienstbarkeit?
> Haben uns denn böse Stunden
> Flammen zubereit?

Flammen, da nur wird gefunden
Trübsal, Kummer, Herzensglut
So die Liebe geben tut.

Wunderseltsam geht es zu:
Wenn die Liebe schafft Unruh
Wird's doch Ruh genannt:
Bei der Lieb ist süßer Schmerzen
Kluger Unverstand
Hart geknüpft mit freiem Herzen,
Trübsal, Kummer, Herzensglut
So die Liebe geben tut.

This is not among the best poetry that Albert put to music, and it is more theatrical than most of the verse of the Königsberg writers. The opening stanza is not very elegant, especially in the second and third lines. The question in the second verse, asking whether it is the 'power of the stars' that forces us into the service of love, continues the mood of self-dramatization, and it is followed by a pair of very flat lines, inquiring whether it is 'evil hours' that have lit these flames of passion. It is strange, the poet reflects in the last stanza, that love, which creates unrest, should be spoken of as peace, and he comments on the 'sweet pains' of love, its 'clever stupidity'. In short, a dramatizing and rhetorical text, with effects obtained by exclamatory statements, exaggerated attitudes, and antithetical juxtaposition. Its refrain and patterned stanzas stamp it as the text of a strophic song. Formally speaking, it is set in this way and printed in the appropriate manner, with the words of only the first verse under the music, and the words of the remaining stanzas printed separately.

Ex. 14     The initial use of repetition is typical of madrigal and cantata. The three appearances of the opening phrase, rising in thirds and suggestive of a notable precedent in the *Lamento* from Monteverdi's opera *Arianne*, intensify and dramatize the feeling. There is a tendency towards recitative, mainly in bars 11 and 12, and coloratura in bars 7–9, where the music 'describes' the lover's sigh. The falling diatonic phrase in bars 10–11, corresponding to the idea of life moving downward to death, is rhetorically expressive, especially in connexion with the rising chromatic figure at *Das in Zittern stets muß schweben!* over a falling bass. The conclusion, with a passage of reiterated quavers derived from the opening bars, is felt more as a dramatic statement than as a melody. This figure is of the kind that invites imitation, and is so treated in the bass at bar 15. This is not, however, imitation merely for reasons of structural convenience but a dramatized relationship of the parts—as when the voice, momentarily changing to a rising crochet figure with chromatic features, is imitated by the bass at bar 16. The two parts have less symmetrical relationship than is often the case with baroque continuo lieder, which is to say that this one is more freely composed. Also, there is hardly a bar which the music, expressively devised for the first verse, is correspondingly appropriate in the others. The impassioned declamation at the words *O der rauhen Grausamkeit!* is hardly in keeping with *Ist es denn der Sternen Kraft*, and seems affected when it comes to *Wunderseltsam geht es zu*. The behaviour of the bass too ceases to be particularly apt, and the pictorialism at *Seufzen* loses its point in the other stanzas. If Albert had taken less care to give the beginning so expressive a musical interpretation, the song as a whole would have been more satisfactory. As it is, the setting of the first verse is indeed impressive, but in its entirety the piece gives an uneasy feeling of aiming at effect. This is partly due to the text, the histrionics of which are more noticeable over three stanzas than in one, but also the passionate and dramatic intensity of the music strains the limits of so restricted a form, illustrating the point that strophic song imposed on the composer a measure of renunciation, if it was not to be pressed in the direction of becoming something else, of assuming qualities that were better treated in cantata. Obviously Albert's interest was aroused by the first verse, which could be detached to form a separate dramatic episode, and in performance it would do him justice to omit the rest.

The many reprints of the *Arien* and the pirated editions testify to Albert's popularity. Similar evidence is provided by the appearance of his songs in other people's collections, like songs copied by Christian Clodius in 1669 and now known as *Das Liederbuch des Leipziger Studenten Clodius*. Of the two of Albert's songs included in it, *Wohl dem, der sich nur läßt begnügen* (II. 9) and *Soll denn schönste Doris ich Ewig leben ohne dich* (II. 13), the first is interesting as an adaptation by Dach of Opitz's *Wohl dem, der weit von hohen Dingen* and in view of the plausible suggestion that Albert's melody was originally a setting of Opitz's poem. Its subsequent appearance in the collection ornately entitled *Gesechste Tugend- und Laster-Rose oder Jungfräulicher Zeitvertreiber, worinnen Allerhand schöne . . . neue Poetische Lieder in bekandte Melodeyen versetzet . . . sind von Constans Holdlieb* (1665) is further evidence of Albert's popularity, especially as this appeared as far away as Nuremberg. Judging by the selections others made from his work, he was loved more for his lieder than his cantatas, or near-cantatas. But he had been anxious to show his mastery of forms which, especially in conjunction with instruments, were more fitting for public and ceremonial occasions. It was for such that his operas were composed, and among the numbers in the *Arien* notable for their cantata features are several in honour of the visiting Elector of Brandenburg.

One consequence of Albert's growing prestige was that more and more he was commissioned, by the nobility, the upper middle-class, and representatives of the higher administration, to provide music for formal occasions, and then he did not usually find the strophic continuo lied appropriate. The type of poetry offered to him by his friends in such quantity must have contributed to his interest in strophic song, but the *Arien* show that texts of this kind could be set in other ways, that for him cantata music did not necessarily demand cantata texts. His own verse was almost entirely simple and strophic, but as a rule he set it in a way that at least was never free from cantata inclinations. One exception would be his setting of *Cynthia mein Leben will sich nicht ergeben*, but the text is an adaptation of Dach's *Lesbia mein Leben Hat sich mir ergeben*, which determined the choice of tune, and, as an *aria gallica*, this is in any case not Albert's own.

Apart from instances where a formal occasion dictated the character of the music, circumstances will often have determined the style. Many a poem will have been set as a simple lied, because it was intended for an evening of informal entertainment for which a particular individual wanted a song to sing. But Albert had ambitions for the satisfaction of which the lied was too modest and too limited, interested though he was in it. Middle-class by birth and upbringing, he was more and more drawn into aristocratic and courtly affairs, and, in conjunction with wider trends of the time, this must be taken into account in considering his equivocal attitude. His influence, paradoxically, was favourable both to the consolidation of the continuo lied, in so far as he produced it in quantity and made it widely popular, and to its disintegration. For the moment the situation was saved by Adam Krieger, in every respect Albert's peer as a composer, who found in the lied his natural medium of expression and remained resolutely loyal to its demands.

# VII

## *The Flowering of Baroque Song*

### ADAM KRIEGER, POET AND COMPOSER

KRIEGER was born in the neighbourhood of Frankfurt an der Oder in 1634 and died at Dresden in 1666. Trained by Scheidt at Halle, he went to Leipzig University, but seems not to have taken his studies very seriously nor to have pursued them very continuously. From about 1650 he played quite a part in the musical life of Leipzig as an organist before moving to Dresden as court organist and music tutor to the reigning family. He unsuccessfully applied for the post of cantor at St. Thomas's while he was in Dresden, using his good relations with court circles to try to gain the appointment.

Elector Johann Georg II (1656–80) was fond of music and of entertainment on a festive scale. He strove to improve the court's musical life, with emphasis on the opera and *Singballett*. It was during his time that the Dresden opera house was built in 1664, two years before Krieger's death. The consequence of these activities was an increase in the influence of Italian opera. This tendency was resisted, notably by Dedekind, who, apart from being a minor poet, was significantly a true and gifted song composer. He had been on the musical establishment since 1654, and it was at his initiative that there was founded a so-called *kleine deutsche Music* with less ambitious functions of its own. With Dedekind as director it brought about a 'strict separation of German and Italian singers'.[1] After Krieger's death, Italian influence increased further under Johann Georg III (1680–91), whose experience of opera in Venice had left its mark on his taste. After the brief rule of Johann Georg IV (1691–4) it culminated in the reign of Friedrich August ('August the Strong'), who died in 1753 and whose succession to the Polish throne, coinciding with his conversion to Catholicism, called for cultural display in the grand manner. It was he who built the *Zwinger*. Its festive function completed with Friedrich August's marriage in 1719, the Italian opera was disbanded in 1720.

Before Krieger moved to Dresden, he was a familiar figure in student

[1] I. Becker-Glauch, *Die Bedeutung der Musik für die Dresdner Hoffeste*, Cassel and Basel, 1951, p. 15.

musical circles in Leipzig, and was, as Mattheson puts it,[1] 'king' of a 'musical society', which met largely for the mutual entertainment of members. Activities of this sort had strong roots in Leipzig, where Schein back in 1626 had published his *Studenten-Schmaus*. Other organizations came into being, the most famous of which was to be Telemann's *collegium musicum*, a forerunner of the one he founded in Hamburg. Many of Krieger's songs were very obviously written for students, like *Seht doch wie der Rheinwein tanzt*. Some of the *Arien*  Ex. 1 appeared during his lifetime, in 1657; an enlarged posthumous edition was published in 1667 under the title *Neue Arien*, and an extension of that edition in 1676. Many of his songs would have been lost but for the initiative of his friend, the poet David Schirmer, who had arrived in Dresden in 1650 and became court poet and librarian, and who was responsible for the 1676 edition. Schirmer, whose *Poetische Rauten-Gepüsche* (Dresden, 1663) contains a poem by Krieger, was able to extend the original collection by seeking out surviving copies from among Krieger's friends, and he added a dedicatory poem mentioning him in the distinguished company of Opitz, Fleming, and Rist.

Krieger certainly was not without poetic talent, as this example shows, clumsy though it tends to be in places:

> Ihr schönen Augen! Ihr heller Glanz!
> Wer wird euch taugen, ihr blendet ganz!
> Ihr klaren Sterne scheint gegen mir,
> Als wie von fernen des Himmels Zier.
>
> Ihr blanken Fackeln beleuchtet mich
> Mit holden Wackeln gar innerlich.
> Ihr Silberstrahlen glänzt ja so sehr,
> Als man kann malen der Sternen Heer.
>
> Ihr güldnen Blitze tanzt auf mich zu,
> Daß ich mich stütze, auf eure Ruh.
> Ihr Augenlider, wenn ihr euch regt,
> So hin und wieder, bin ich erlegt.
>
> Ihr Sonnen wecket mich wieder auf,
> Ich war verstecket, vor eurem Lauf,
> Ihr schnellen Boten der Liebeslust
> Knüpft manchen Knoten in meiner Brust.
>
> Ihr süßen Blicke löst wiederum
> Was eure Stricke geknüpft im Grimm.
> Ihr Wunderkerzen, wie steckt ihr an,
> Daß man die Schmerzen kaum dulden kann.

[1] *Critica Musica*, ii, 1725, p. 253.

Ihr lieben Lichter verblendet oft
Viel Angesichter, ganz unverhofft.
Zünd't an, ihr Flammen, gleich alle Welt,
Laßt nur beisammen, was mir gefällt.

Zwar viel zu wenig bin ich für euch,
Wär ich schon König, und hätt' ein Reich.
Wiewohl ich brenne in voller Glut
Und fühl und kenne mein armes Blut.

Was kann ich machen? Das Venuskind
Durch euer Lachen mich so entzünd't.
Ich bin geboren zur Sterblichkeit
Und ganz verloren bei dieser Zeit.

Weil ich muß lieben, was göttlich ist,
Wie soll ich üben die süße Lust?
Ich muß vergehen durch ihren Strahl,
Ich kann kaum stehen in meiner Qual.

Wie will es werden, wenn mich sofort
Auf dieser Erden die Lieb ermord't?
Ich kann nicht sehen, wie mir hierbei,
Es mag geschehen, zu helfen sei.

Denn wer an Götter sich hat vergafft,
Wird als ein Spötter dahin gerafft.
Nun, soll ich sterben, so hab ich doch,
Vor allen Erben, den Vorzug noch,

Daß um was Göttlichs ich fort gemußt,
Und nicht was Spöttlichs, erstickt die Brust.
Drum ist mirs 'gangen wie Icaro:
Ich wollte prangen, und sterbe so.

The theme is conventional down to the details of phraseology and metaphor, as can be seen by reference to a poem in Mühlpforth's posthumous *Teutsche Gedichte* (1698):

Ihr schönen Augen ihr,
Ich fühle Glut,
Und eure Wunderzier
Erhitzt mein Blut.
Die angenehme Freundlichkeit,
So süße Blicke streut,
Macht mich erfreut.

Ihr Fackeln meiner Seel,
Ich bin entbrannt,
Aus eurer schwarzen Höhl
Und Diamant

Kommt mir der süße Gegenschein,
Daß ich verliebt muß sein
In meiner Pein.

Ihr Flammen meiner Lust
Wie brennt ihr so?
Wie macht ihr meine Brust
So herzlich froh!
Leitsterne in der Paradeiß,
Eu'r so geliebtes Weiß,
Das macht mir heiß.

Strahlt Kerzen in der Nacht,
Weist mir die Bahn.
Ich bin ja eurer Pracht
Ganz untertan.
Die Sonne muß sich nicht entziehn,
Sonst wird mein Leben fliehn,
Und ganz verblühn.

Ach küßt ich diesen Strahl
In heißer Brunst,
Der mir teils schenket Qual,
Teils süße Gunst;
Ich schwöre, daß ich sterbe so,
Und bin in eurer Loh
Von Herzen froh.

*Schöne Augen, süße Blicke, Fackeln, ich sterbe so*—these words and phrases appear in exactly the same guise in Krieger's poem, *Wunderzier* and *in meiner Pein* have their near-equivalents (*Wunderkerzen, in meiner Qual*), and the theme itself is too obviously similar to need comment. Mühlpforth belongs to the trend associated with Hofmannswaldau and the Second Silesian School, and its verse-form and other features make his poem characteristic of the 'galant' phase of the later baroque lyric. He was born in Breslau in 1639 and finally settled there, and died in 1681. In the meantime one episode in his life took him in 1657 to Leipzig with the intention of studying medicine. In view of this it is reasonable to suspect that his poem, despite its different style, may have been influenced by Krieger's.

Krieger's poem illustrates once again how in baroque verse the simultaneity of joy and sorrow, a spontaneous element in folk-song, becomes the object of reflection and analysis. As with Regnart, the poses are as much for the benefit of an audience by implication present to admire the virtuosity of the poet's feeling and of his art, as for that of the imagined lady—though she too would be expected to be

impressed by this as well. In Krieger's song these sophistications are
transferred to the sphere of informal music-making as among students
and associated with a very singable tune, without coloratura, and
moving by easy intervals, major third or perfect fifth.

Essentially this is a dance-song and, like most baroque dances, it
is binary; as a rule each section of a dance comprised eight bars or
a multiple of eight. The eight bars of the melody form the first section,
the second is the ritornello, with one bar missing—the incompleteness
serving to imply continuation and return to the beginning with the
following stanza. There is something corresponding to this in the text
too. Substituting feet for bars, each pair of lines provides two sections
of eight, with a corresponding rhyming scheme, *aabb*. The rhythm
of the words, moreover, subtly accommodates itself to the musical
rhythm, or is shaped by it. In common-time dances the first beat of
the bar was usually slightly stronger than the third, just as in reading
the poem the first syllable of *schönen* would carry a little more weight
than the first syllable of *Augen*. (For purposes of this comparison, the
unstressed first syllable of the line is treated as the up-beat as at the end
of a bar.) The same is true of the first syllable of *heller* as compared with
the accent on *Glanz*, and so forth. This serves to reduce the jog-trot of
the iambics, and so does the way in the song the unaccented syllables
are more heavily stressed than would be the case if the text were read.
The reason is that the length of a note influences its degree of stress:
'a difference in temporal duration between two notes is more noticeable than a difference in accentuation; musical "prosody", so to speak,
is always quantitative, not qualitative'.[1] The unstressed syllables in
the setting are often as long as the stressed ones; the final syllable of
*schönen* falls on a crotchet, like the stressed syllable on either side
of it.

The genesis of this poem, therefore, was clearly conditioned by
musical experience, and from this point of view there is a further
aspect to be noticed. The text divides into two halves, each with a
character of its own. In the first the poet addresses his lady, and this
is distinguished by its frequent metaphors, at the beginning of most of
the first and third lines of every stanza. This section suggests action
and physical movement; the eyes *blenden*, the *güldne Blitze* of her
eyes *tanzen auf mich zu*, they are suns that *wecken mich*. Its prevailing
character is narrative and dramatic. In the second section the metaphors cease, the very first word (*zwar*) implies a change, reflection on

---

[1] W. H. Auden, Introduction to *An Elizabethan Song Book*, London, 1957, p. vii.

what has happened, and the contemplative *Ich* occurs fourteen times. This division could be compared with the operatic practice, whereby dramatic features usually coloured the recitative, which 'tells the story', the ensuing aria being inward and reflective.

Reference to the text has shown that behind its essentially popular character there is a debt to a more serious and sophisticated type of verse, and the same is true of the music. Even if public concert halls had existed at this time, it is not there that this song would have been performed, but in ale-house and tavern. Yet a too superficial acquaintance with it would conceal qualities with more refined associations. In the poem we noticed the presence of an implied audience together with features derived from the dance, and a relationship analogous to that between recitative and aria. As to the instrumental section, it is not enough to say that Krieger's ritornelli 'are only evidence of the use of these songs in a social gathering or a *Collegium*'. It is true that people would have taken a poor view of a composer of songs for *collegia musica*, if he had given the better instrumentalists present nothing better to do than sit and listen to a singer. Plenty of Krieger's ritornelli admittedly require no more highfalutin explanation than this, and Krieger might well have been content with it. Since, however, there is hardly a verse where gesture and mime could not be imagined as adding rhetorical, dramatizing effect to the feeling and situation, and since the poem thus impels the imagination towards visual representation, the ritornello allows itself to be thought of as an implied ballet, an undanced dance. Ballet 'shows the body's movements transferred from a real pattern of physical behaviour into an ideal analogue of feeling',[1] and some of Krieger's ritornelli are important enough to illustrate this principle, like those in *Adonis Tod*, the first expressing Aphrodite's fears about the fate of Adonis on the hunt, the second her anguished realization that he has been slain by a wild boar. They suggest too a visual representation of a funeral procession, thus combining between them the functions of an 'expressive formula image' and a 'representational image'.[2]

If one aspect of *Ihr schönen Augen!* is as a song for purposes of informal entertainment, another is characterized by its intensity, or feigned intensity, of feeling. But its passion is held within the limits of balance and proportion, and in its wider implications this is a characteristically baroque feature, so that one of the forms dearest to

[1] R. Peacock, *The Art of Drama*, London, 1957, p. 248 n.
[2] Ibid., p. 38.

the hearts of baroque composers was that which builds an expressive, even passionate, line over a recurring and stable pattern in the bass— 'divisions on a ground', passacaglia, chaconne. The greatest of Bach's keyboard works, the *Goldberg Variations*, exemplifies this principle. A poet of a later age, struggling to 'tame his monstrous fantasies',[1] remarked cryptically that all problems of literary creation could be related to the figured bass—'Ich glaube, daß im Generalbaß die wichtigsten Aufschlüsse über die Dichtkunst enthalten sind.'[2] Was Kleist perhaps thinking of this controlling element in baroque music? The recurring harmonic structure of *Ihr schönen Augen!* is of such limited and indeterminate character as to be virtually neutral, and upon it is built a vocal line communicating, stanza by stanza, ever new variations of the theme. The text of the song is ornate to a degree now felt to be slightly absurd, but in alliance with the music the result is something lying deep in the baroque, the expressive interplay of subjective feeling and objective order—just as in the text human passion is brought into relationship with the universe, with the 'army of unalterable law', a common enough theme in the seventeenth century:

> Man is all symmetry,
> Full of proportion, one limb to another,
>     And all to all the world besides:
> Each part may call the furthest brother:
> For head with foot has private amity,
>     And both with moons and tides.

It is typical of Krieger that, just as his strophic continuo lieder can achieve a remarkable range of expression within this restricted form, his pieces more in the style of cantata are restrained by principles characteristic of the lied. His cantatas are, therefore, more song-like than Albert's, though they may have been intended for stage performance, perhaps as *Singballette*.

Thus, if the text of *Adonis Tod* is arranged in its metrical pattern as a poem, the result is as follows:

> Wo muß der schöne Jäger sein,
> Adonis meine Seele?
> Um den ich in verliebter Pein
> Mich ofte plag und quäle?

---

[1] M. Hamburger, *Reason and Energy*, London, 1957, p. 142.
[2] Bibliographisches Institut edition of Kleist's *Briefe*, ed. G. Minde-Pouet, i. 262.

Er eilt dem bloßen Wilde nach
Und ich desselben Schatten.
Sein Herz und Sinnen sein die Schmach,
So mich sonst bei sich hatten.

Ich habe seinen Hut gesehn
Und mehr von ihm im Walde.
O Himmel, laß es doch geschehn,
Daß ich ihn finde balde.

O bittre Pein!
Über die wohl nichts kann sein.
Ein wildes Schwein hat den erschlagen,
Ach! den ich ewig muß beklagen.
O Angst und Not!
Ach! Adonis ist tot!
Mein Adonis ist tot!

O süßes Herz!
Sonst ein Scherz und nun mein Schmerz,
Muß dich ein grimmig Tier ertöten.
Ach! und die schöne Zier erröten,
O Angst und Not!
Ach! Adonis ist tot!
Mein Adonis ist tot!

O herbe Qual!
Die mir als ein Donnerstrahl,
Das Mark in Beinen ganz versehret,
Ach! und des Herzens Blut verzehret.
O Angst und Not!
Ach! Adonis ist tot!
Mein Adonis ist tot!

In this unimpressive text three stanzas of one metrical type are balanced by three of another. The first would meet the demands of a simple strophic lied. Though the last three have lines of varying length, the variation is consistent and yields a common pattern. The metrical latitude in the second half is obviously prompted by the freedom it offers the composer, and characteristic of this part are emotional outbursts which could provide the opportunity for extremely affective music.

Ex. 17 The setting of the first three stanzas does not overstep the limits of a strophic lied, with ritornello, neither does the opening of the second section. But soon the simpler metre begins to be influenced by one of a different and more drawn-out kind, and immediately afterwards the metrical flow is interrupted, as the *Ach!* claims its expressive due. From this point repetition occurs, and there are moments when one may be tempted to expect recitative. There is an imaginative use of the liberties possible outside the strict limits of the strophic lied, as in the way in lines 3 and 4 of the penultimate stanza a lengthening of the last bar subtly alters the anticipated pattern. The change is made all the more effective when at the beginning of the phrase the *Ach!* is allowed to occupy a whole beat, instead of merely an unstressed quaver, as would be the case if the exact pattern were respected.

The following text is written with greater metrical freedom:

> Fleug, Psyche, fleug,
> Cupido will nicht mehr dein eigen sein.
> Hier hat er sich in diesen hellen Augen
> Der zarten Braut
> Ein Wohnhaus aufgebaut.
> Dir, o schönste Zier,
> Erwirbt er nur allein dergleichen Ehr
> Und schätzt dich gleich der wundervollen Psyche,
> Von der er neulich wiche.
> Wo nun Cupido sitzet
> Und in der Stirne blitzet,
> Da muß die süße Liebespein
> Voll Hitz und Feuer sein.
>
> Freilich, freilich ist die Glut,
> So dahier in eurem Mut
> Und in allen Adern brennet,
> Von der Venus angezünd't,
> Weil sie, gar zu liebes Kind,
> Gleich nach euren Augen rennet.
>
> Hier laßt ihr die Liebesflamm
> Eurem liebsten Bräutigam,
> Gleich nach seinem Herzen schießen.
> Er hingegen lacht und denkt,
> Was ihn itzund heimlich kränkt,
> Bald vollkommen zu genießen.
>
> So genieße frisch und frei
> Deine Lust, du schönes zwei,
> Und erlange dein Verlangen,
> Was der Himmel Gutes gibt,
> Sei in dich zugleich verliebt,
> So kannst du vergnüget prangen.
>
> Wir wünschen euch und eurem Herzen
> Ein recht erfreulich Liebesscherzen,

Ein Glücke von des Himmels Höhe,
Daß alles Trauern von euch gehe
Ein süß und angenehmes Lieben,
Das alle Welt so oft getrieben,
Ein Herz und Sinn und eine Seele
So lange wir in dieser Höhle
Die hochgeschätzten Himmelsgaben
Mit Freuden können bei uns haben.

Fleug, Psyche, fleug, &c.

Of the thirteen lines of the opening section, two are trochaic, but, with the exception of the first line, which begins with a dactyl (or, if one prefers, a spondee), the remainder are all iambic, though of varying lengths. One has five feet, two have four, one has two, and the others have three. The first three lines do not rhyme, but a clear-cut rhyming scheme (*aabbccddee*) begins at the fourth line. During the second half of this opening section a pattern of three-stressed lines establishes itself, interrupted only by the penultimate line. Thus, after a fairly free start, it moves towards a more or less regular prosodic pattern, and its conclusion settles down into what could well become a strophic arrangement. There follow three stanzas of equal lines with a uniform metre. The following section, it is true, breaks this pattern; it has more lines than the three preceding verses, and changes from iambs to trochees. But the lines are of uniform length, the metre is consistent, and so is the rhyming scheme.

It has been said that this text marks a 'significant disruption of the simple strophic form . . . that dominates the lyrical poetry of the time', that it is 'a decisive step towards "madrigalian" poetry'.[1] What must not be overlooked, however, is that, while Krieger allows himself freedom to vary the metre, the length of the lines, and the rhyming,
**Ex. 18** the predominating feature is a very marked tendency towards symmetrical order, and the music confirms this. Despite the flexibility of the first lines of the text, the setting adheres to a fairly regular metrical pattern in triple time, with dance features. A sudden written-in *adagio*, contrasting with the *presto* at the end, and the coloratura at *Feuer* serving to provide a dramatic conclusion are among the few features in the music that really require reference to cantata. The three six-line stanzas in the middle, like part of the earlier example, could form a strophic continuo lied, with ritornelli, in its own right, and there is no recitative.

[1] E. Schmitz, op. cit., p. 226.

Ziegler's treatise *Von den Madrigalen, einer schönen und zur Musik bequemsten Art Verse*, inspired by a letter from Schütz in 1653 urging the value of madrigal texts for composers, had appeared four years before the first edition of Krieger's *Arien*. The first section of *Fleug, Psyche, fleug*, could be used to illustrate the kind of poem that Ziegler had in mind. It falls within the limits he laid down of not less than five lines or more than fifteen or sixteen. The short lines do not meet his requirement of a minimum of six syllables, but the longer ones do not exceed his maximum of eleven. He said that all lines need not rhyme, though in his examples, as here, many do. While it is possible that Krieger was influenced by Ziegler's treatise, other factors too must be taken into account. Schirmer's *Poetische Rauten-Gepüsche*, published at Dresden in 1663, appeared after Ziegler's work, but contains madrigals of earlier date, written even before Ziegler had published his views. What led Schirmer to write them? At least by about 1622 it was not uncommon in France to insert madrigals into ballets, and under French influence works of this kind began to find favour in Germany. In 1655 *Das Ballett des Atlas* was performed at the Dresden court, combining, in the different sections of its several *entrées*, ballet, madrigal, and strophic song. The text, by Schirmer, is included in the *Poetische Rauten-Gepüsche*. Krieger was a close friend of Schirmer, and he must have known about performances of this sort. *Fleug, Psyche, fleug*, begins with what is virtually a madrigal, includes the equivalent of a lied, and the ritornelli correspond to the danced sections. This analogy would strengthen the possibility that the work was the text of a *Singballett*, in which case the ritornelli would have accompanied the dancers.

Krieger's *Arien* show sophisticated, courtly influences penetrating the entertainment requirements of a less refined audience, middle-class in the main, with students conspicuous. They played a particularly important part in cultural and social life in and around Leipzig, reflected in Schoch's *Comoedia vom Studenten-Leben*, published there in 1657, portraying the more riotous sides of their activities. It was nowhere more true than in Leipzig that only in song did baroque poetry become 'popular'. But this was not always a matter for satisfaction, especially when its popularity extended to a more plebeian public. Schoch, a poet and composer, complained about the fate of Schirmer's poems, which Stolle in 1654 had set to music in his *Singende Rosen*. Intended for the entertainment of his friends and acquaintances, he lamented that in so short a time they had 'fallen into low company'. He regretted that his own *Immer hin, fahr immer hin*, had been heard so much that 'now no tailor's apprentice can darn a pair of stockings in his workshop, and no locksmith's lad can fetch himself a mug of beer from the cellar, without singing or whistling it'.[1] If Krieger had lived long enough to observe the growth of his own popularity, it looks, from one's impression of the man, as if he would have reacted in a different way. In any case we remember his *Arien* as the most perfect union of poetry and song ever achieved in the secular lied of the German baroque, but nearer his own time some thought him above all as one whose very popularity had debased the lied and made it merely common:

> Seit des edlen Kriegers Sachen
> Sich der Welt zu kundbar machen,
> Wird der schönste Klang gemein.[2]

[1] Quoted by A. Schering, *Musikgeschichte Leipzigs*, Leipzig, 1926, p. 359.
[2] Ibid., p. 360.

# VIII

## Music in the Service of Poetry

### JOHANN RIST AND HIS COMPOSERS

THAT the balance between poetry and music exemplified in Krieger's *Arien* might sooner or later be disturbed by the desire for greater freedom of musical expression will be obvious enough, a process to be reflected in due course in the shift of interest from lied to aria. For the moment our concern is with an opposite development, with the way not poetry but music could be made to play the subordinate role.

Rist's first volume of poetry (*Musa Teutonica*, 1634) achieved considerable success and was followed, in 1638, 1646, and 1652, by the *Poetischer Lust-Garte*, the *Poetischer Schauplatz*, and the *Neüer Teütscher Parnaß*, all published in or near Hamburg. Following Opitz, and schooled on the fashionable models of foreign literatures, Rist had set himself the task of enriching German literature with the fruits of the new learning, sonnet, ode, epigram, and elegy, and in the *Musa Teutonica* he praises Opitz as the person 'who showed us how we too in our language could have Petrarchs, Ariostos, and Ronsards'. He refers obliquely to Opitz also when in the *Poetischer Lust-Garte* he writes: 'But I know that I have ... diligently striven to pay attention to the rules of our prosody, and have particularly wished also to write clearly (*klar, deutlich*), and in a way that everyone could understand.' The principle stated in the last part of this remark will be seen to have some significance regarding Rist's views on music suitable for his verse, and it is worth drawing attention to Opitz's remark in the *Buch von der deutschen Poeterey*: 'Elegance (*Zierlichkeit*) demands that the words should be pure and clear (*deutlich*).'[1] Rist's adherence to this principle made it *a priori* unlikely that he would be willing to countenance a relationship between his poetry and music other than one in which the poetry should be the dominant partner.

Of the volumes mentioned, the first more or less coincides with Rist's appointment to a clerical living at Wedel, and one senses in his

---

[1] Ed. cit., p. 24.

preface a note of self-defence against those who may be assumed to have criticized him for indulging in the amorous frivolities of secular poetry. He replied, in the *Musa Teutonica*, that among his honoured predecessors were men who had not felt it amiss to 'sugar' their work with poems about the delights of love. But in the *Poetischer Schauplatz* he recognized that 'an upright poet should certainly not make use of such heathen and vulgar verse', and in the *Neüer Teütscher Parnaß* that 'in writing verse we should not use the lies, the accursed idols, and the vices of the heathen, just as there is no need to sail from Germany to India'. This was a general and much-discussed problem, illustrated by Johann Heermann, who used classical mythology a good deal in his Latin poetry, but kept it out of his religious German verse. Athens and Jerusalem, he said in the foreword to the *Poetische Erquickstunden* (1656), have nothing in common. At any rate Rist seems to have stopped writing secular poetry under persuasion from friends who thought some of his themes a little improper for a clergy-man. In any case he was increasingly concerned with his pastoral duties and anxious to enrol poetry in their service. Again there is a comparison with Heermann, who had explained in the *Andächtige Kirch-Seufftzer* (1616) that his object was to inspire his flock to prayer by reading to them rhymed versions of Bible passages after the sermon, and his *Sontags- und Fest-Evangelia* (1636) had a similar purpose.

Between the *Poetischer Lust-Garte* and the *Poetischer Schauplatz* the first part of Rist's *Himlische Lieder* appeared in 1641, followed by numerous other religious collections. The *Neüer Teütscher Parnaß* was the last secular volume he himself published, but friends of his published two more, *Des Dafnis aus Cimbrien Galatee* and *Des edlen Dafnis aus Cimbrien Besungene Florabella* (Hamburg, 1642 and 1651). Both are in the fashionable stream of pastoral poetry, dealing with conventional themes, and particularly the first attained considerable popularity. Pairs of shepherds declare their love, swear eternal devotion, or, as circumstances demand, lament the prospect of separation. Some of the poems in the *Poetischer Schauplatz* are described as fitting tunes from *Galatee*, indicating that this too had made its mark. Further evidence is the appearance in Switzerland in 1656 of four-part arrangements of the songs ('in order that they can be sung or played on instruments'), but the melodies were left unaltered, 'because everybody knows them'.

Rist's interest in music as a practising amateur is referred to in the preface to the *Seelengespräche*, and he followed with interest the affairs of the Hamburg *collegium musicum*. We know him as a composer from a few pieces in his secular volumes, and he also adapted other people's tunes. Schütz called on him on his way to Denmark, the occasion that prompted Rist's well-known dactylic poem *Seh ich nicht kommen den trefflichen Sänger*, though by this time his literary fame was sufficient to explain Schütz's motives—and enough to enable Rist to secure the collaboration of a considerable number of composers.

With few exceptions these were minor figures. Some were connected with Hamburg, including three organists (Jacob Schultze, Heinrich Scheidemann, and Jacob Kortkamp) and a cantor (Thomas Selle). The Hamburg composers included also Peter Meier and Johann Schop. The latter had been on the establishment of the court at Wolfenbüttel, and, after intervals in Denmark and Paris, had gone to Hamburg in 1621. He could write chorale-like melodies greatly to Rist's taste, and he also had a name as a violinist. At the time Rist's praise of him in the *Himlische Lieder* as a man 'whose high intelligence, excellent art, and experience in the noble art of song are well known throughout Europe' would not have been regarded as absurd. Schop was ambitious and, probably growing impatient with the restraints that Rist imposed, after a certain stage he played no further part. Less is known about Martin Coler, who seems to have been for a time in Hamburg around 1661, and was a member of the *Elbenschwanenorden*. Heinrich Pape, an organist, lived at near-by Altona, and Christian Flor, particularly associated with Rist's *Seelenparadies*, was an organist of repute at Lüneburg; two suites of his survive, so does part of a St. Matthew Passion. A letter of his to Rist is interesting as showing that Rist usually only provided his composers with the first verse of a text, and also that Flor had mild contempt for simple music such as Rist required. Michael Jacobi, a cantor from Lüneburg, earned Rist's praise, through usually obeying his instructions, in contrast to Flor who allowed himself tonal and rhythmic latitude, and occasional chromaticism. Another collaborator, from farther afield, was Gottlieb Staden, an organist at Nuremberg, composer of the music for *Seelewig*, the opera in Harsdörffer's *Frauenzimmer Gesprechspiele*. More important than all these was Hammerschmidt, whose *Weltliche Oden* owed its popularity mainly to tuneful numbers like the setting of Fleming's poem *Nirgends hin als auf den Mund*. The predominance of organists in this list is striking, though Rist was not prejudiced against the collaboration of the cantors. Jacob Schwieger, whose *Liebesgrillen* was published in Hamburg in 1654, felt it advantageous to stress that the tunes were by people 'skilled in the noble art of song and organ music'. Some of Rist's composers were among Schwieger's collaborators, and one of them, Coler, also contributed to Stieler's *Die geharnischte Venus* (Hamburg, 1660).

In his earlier collections Rist seems to have regarded music as little more than a graceful addition to his verse, as in this example:

Dorinde, du prächtigst auf Erden
Von Tugend, Zucht, Schönheit, Gebärden,
Laß mich deinen Diener sein:
Ich lauf ihr nach Mit Weh und Ach,
Schau an mein Herz, Das voller Schmerz
In Flammen steht! Kein Tag vergeht,
Ich seufze nach dir mein Täubelein.

Dorinde, du Perle der Jugend,
Du edelster Spiegel der Tugend,
Du mein erwünschtes Gut:
Ich lauf ihr nach Mit Weh und Ach,
Schau an mein Leid, Das jederzeit
Mich Armen quält, Weil ich erwählt,
Die Phoebus selber beneiden tut.

Dorinde, du Bild der Göttinnen,
Du schönste von allen Schäf'rinnen,
Du trefflichste Himmelszier:
Ich lauf ihr nach Mit Weh und Ach,
Schau mein Gesicht, Wie mir zerbricht
Herz, Mut und Sinn! Mein Geist fleucht hin,
Weil ich nicht stets mag sein bei dir.

Dorinde, Prinzessin der Frauen,
Wann werd ich einst fröhlich dich schauen,
Wann komm ich zu dir hin?
Ich lauf ihr nach Mit Weh und Ach,
Wenn soll's denn sein, O Täubelein,
Daß du zuletzt Mich einst ergetzt?
Ich rufe: Ade, mein Schäferin.

Ex. 19 If, as could well have been the case, Schop was the composer, this setting does him credit, without substantiating the view that he stands comparison with Krieger. The composer clearly felt some obligation to give due effect to the predominantly rhythmic features of the text, and beyond that does little more than attempt to convey its playful excitation. The music gracefully embellishes the words in the first verse, but, spread over the remainder, loses some of its interest, as it continues to exploit rhythmical effects obvious enough in the text.

Rist's religious verse brought a change in his attitude to the content of his poetry, and a more utilitarian view about the function of music. In his first volume of religious verse, the *Himlische Lieder*, he points out that the melodies aim at being 'simple' and 'clear', capable of being sung by ordinary people. Anyone, he adds, who finds them too simple should not blame Schop, who acted on instructions. Schop had to modify his natural style for the purpose, and he took a little time to achieve the desired degree of simplicity. In the first two parts there is occasional counterpoint, but not from the third part onwards. Schop's music achieved the intended results, so that, introducing in 1648 *Der zu seinem allerheiligsten Leiden und Sterben hingeführte und an das Kreütz geheftete Christus Jesus* (with tunes by Pape, who had set most of the earlier *Galatee*), Rist could boast that Schop's melodies were being sung even by children. In the foreword to the *Neuer himlischer Lieder sonderbahres Buch* (1651) Rist said that those 'inexperienced in the noble art of song' could sing the texts to familiar hymn tunes, but this did not mean that he ceased to demand simplicity from his composers. In all his religious songs dissonance and rhythmic variation are exceptional, and as a rule each syllable is set to a single note. The result, not surprisingly, is often rather like a chorale, as in the case of *O Ewigkeit du Donnerwort*.                                                    Ex. 20

In the earlier example, Rist's use of the dactyl illustrates a new development in German verse in so far as Opitz had, in general, allowed only iambs and trochees. Opitz's views corresponded to those of the English theorists. Campion (*Observations*, 1602)[1] thought the dactyl an 'attempt altogether against the nature of our language. For both the concourse of our monosillables make our verse unapt to slide and also, if we examine our polysillables, we shall finde few of them, by reason of their heaviness, willing to serve in place of a Dactile.' ('The natural course of most English verses', William Webbe had said in his *Discourse of English Poetrie* (1586), 'seemeth to run upon the old Iambic stroake.')[2] In due course in Germany Buchner made influential propaganda on behalf of the dactyl. His *Anleitung zur deutschen Poeterey* did not appear (posthumously) until 1665, but its author had been expressing views on the subject for some years as professor at Wittenberg. Buchner's insistence that the dactyl was

---

[1] G. Gregory Smith (ed.), *Elizabethan Critical Essays*, Oxford, 1904, i. 333.
[2] Ibid., p. 273.

necessary to accommodate certain types of polysyllabic words desirable and legitimate in German was not the only issue involved, and the vehemence with which the matter was debated in the *Fruchtbringende Gesellschaft* shows the feeling aroused. Among Buchner's allies was Schottel, who in his *Ausführliche Arbeit von der Teutschen Haubt Sprache* calls the dactyl 'one of the sweetest kinds of rhyme in the German language'.

Evidence suggests that in Germany music may well have helped to predispose the ear in favour of the dactyl. Hassler, as we have seen, imposes sometimes a dactylic feature upon a consistently iambic text, as at the beginning of the first line of the piece analysed in Chapter III. A similar instance, matched by many other examples, is provided by Demant's setting, in his *Ander Theil neuer deutscher Lieder* (1615), of the line:

> Zart schönes Bild an Tugend reich,

which, apart from the setting, would be scanned as a series of iambic feet, but, with the music in one's ear, one could accustom oneself to the impression of the first three syllables as forming a dactyl. In Rist's *Hausmusik* the iambic lines:

> Herr, unser Arzt und treuer Hort,
> Der du durch dein allmächtigs Wort

are to a tune that similarly treats the beginning of each of these lines as dactyls. In the sixteenth century dance-rhythms in music, particularly in Italy, often had dactylic features. Many frottola tunes begin with a dactylic figure (minim–crotchet–crotchet), which was frequent also in the *chanson* and became a stock opening for the *canzone*. Fleming's early use of the dactyl in his poem *O liebliche Wangen* is probably explained by its derivation from an Italian dance-tune. A well-known folk-song begins with iambs and goes into dactyls:

> Es ist ein Schnitter, heißt der Tod,
> Hat Gewalt vom großen Gott:
> Heut wetzt er das Messer,
> Es schneidt schon viel besser:
> Bald wird er drein schneiden,
> Wir müssen nur leiden;
> Hüt dich, schöns Blümelein!

—the verbal equivalent of the pairing, familiar in the sixteenth century, of a slow duple-time dance and a faster one in triple-time, as with pavanes and galliards. A text written to a triple-time dance need not be dactylic, of course, as can be seen by reference to a galliard of Demants's[1] provided with the words:

> Annalein, höchster Schatz auf Erden.

But it is not long before the text tends to become dactylic under the pressure of the music, as at the lines:

> Ach wie du wilt, herziges Bild,
> freundlich und mild. . . .

Rist himself was alive to the way this could happen, as one sees from some remarks of his in one volume (1642) of the *Himlische Lieder*: 'I remember what happened many years ago with this kind of verse. For example, when a gay saraband . . . came into my hands and I was asked to write words to its jolly tune, it turned out that what I produced was in dactyls, although until then I had never seen nor heard of a line in this metre.' English experience confirms the connexion: 'The coranto and sarabande invaded England in King James' reign: and more and more lyrics were written in triple metre. . . .'[2]

The context of Rist's remarks, twenty-three years before the appearance of Buchner's *Anleitung zur deutschen Poeterey*, is a discussion of when it is appropriate to use 'dactylic anapaestic, and similar metres', and when it is not. He finds that they no longer appeal to him 'for the treatment of celestial themes', because 'a soul occupied with thoughts of God should not approach its Redeemer and the heavenly Jerusalem with leaps and jumps, but rather with sighs and longing'. He has used them himself, he admits, and they 'give a special delight to the reader at the right time and in the right place'. The dactyl, however, 'has a modest value and only in connexion with love-songs and pastoral songs, and in other secular contexts. . . . But for poems about God and Heaven I for my part . . . never wish to use so light and dance-like a type of verse.' Schütz too associated dactylic verse with gaiety and joy, and, believing it particularly suitable for

---

[1] Printed as an appendix to R. Kade, 'Christoph Demant, 1567–1643', *Vierteljahrschrift für Musikwissenschaft*, vi, 1890, pp. 537–8.

[2] W. Maynard in *Modern Language Review*, li, 1956, p. 263, reviewing *Musique et Poésie au XVIe siècle* (*Colloques Internationaux du Centre National de la Recherche Scientifique: Sciences Humaines. V*), Paris, 1954. Pattison (op. cit., p. 181) makes much the same point: '. . . the predominating measure in all Elizabethan verse continued to be stress-iambic. In the early seventeenth century, however, triple resolutions became more and more frequent, until after the Restoration triple rhythms were very common indeed in lyric verse. . . . The increased fondness for triple rhythms appears to be connected with developments in the dance.'

musical setting, begged his librettist, Buchner, to employ it for the jollification at the end of *Orpheus* (1638).[1] Morhof (*Unterricht von der Teutschen Sprache und Poesie*, 1700) also denied its suitability for serious themes, regarding it as 'feminine' and 'buffoon-like', though Barthold Feind (*Gedancken von der Opera*, 1708) rather strangely thought it apt to express *fureur*.[2]

Ex. 21    In the text, for example, of a song from *Florabella* Rist concentrates all the interest on metre, leaving Peter Meier little scope beyond giving this a simple and appropriate musical effect. The same is true Ex. 22 of Rist's own setting of *Der Herzliebenden Floridans lustiges Herbst- und Liebes-Leid*. In these secular songs music is thus made subservient to the poetry. This is also the case with his religious songs, but for a different reason. With the latter it was because its function was to familiarize the public with the verse and its message, while in the former the poetry was too much interested in aural effects to leave music much room to make a characteristic contribution of its own. But Rist's religious verse too could have an imposing sound, like *O Ewigkeit du Donnerwort*, the sonority of which gives it a wider appeal than only as a statement of belief. Rist's dactylic verse pushes this a stage farther. Relieved of the distractions of weighty themes, it appeals wholly to the ear, and in the most obvious way possible, through the rhythms of dance.

When German poetry was technically less accomplished, it had relied on music to provide metre and rhythm, and then, helped by the influence of music, it learnt to include these among its own resources. The point had now come when poetry would more and more seek its justification less in what it said than in what it sounded like. Poetry itself would sing and dance. What contribution was music then to make? The question, an important one, is best answered by the work of Philipp Zesen on the one hand and of the Nuremberg poets on the other.

---

[1] Quoted by H. J. Moser, *Heinrich Schütz. Sein Leben und sein Werk*, Cassel, 1936, p. 154.
[2] Quoted by I. Schreiber, *Dichtung und Musik der deutschen Opernarien, 1680–1700* (Diss.), Bottrop i.W., 1934, p. 13 n.

# IX

## *Poetry as Music*

### PHILIPP ZESEN AND THE NUREMBERG POETS

ZESEN, like Rist, was the son of a clergyman, and he was intended
for the Church. He went to a grammar school at Halle, studied under
Buchner at Wittenberg, and in 1642 went to Hamburg, where he
founded a literary society, the *Deutschgesinnte Genossenschaft*. He was
a restless and adventurous person, exceptional in baroque Germany
as a man of letters who did not follow another full-time profession.
Some thought him vain and conceited, and Rist branded him as
a vagrant, a man without honour, and he was just as bitter in his
criticisms of Rist.

Some of his verse is coloured by the Protestant hymn, but in the
main his poetry relies on alliteration, assonance, internal rhymes, echo
devices, and rhythmical effects:

> Halt, du schöner Morgenstern, bleibe fern
> Und du güldne Nachtlaterne
> Halt der weißen Pferde Lauf itzund auf!
> Steht ein wenig still, ihr Sterne!
>
> Gönne mir die süße Ruh, Sonne du,
> Laß uns doch der Liebe pflegen,
> Laß den kühlen Reif und Tau auf der Au
> Noch ein wenig meinetwegen!
>
> Ist doch meine Liebste mir Sonn und Zier,
> Die mich itzund in den Armen,
> In den zarten Armen weiß, die mein Preis
> Und mich also läßt erwarmen.
>
> Und du wunderschönes Licht, die ich nicht
> Nach der Gnüge kann beschreiben,
> Laß den hellen Augenschein bei mir sein,
> Bis der Tag die Nacht will treiben!
>
> Ach entschlage dich ja nicht, schönes Licht,
> Dieser Lust in deiner Jugend,
> Brauche deiner Lieblichkeit und der Zeit,
> Schadt es doch nicht deiner Tugend!

Laß uns immer freudig sein; Nacht und Wein
Reizen uns itzund zum Lieben,
Denn wenn Liebe, Wein und Nacht uns anlacht,
Kann uns Langmut nicht betrüben.

A poem in praise of the *Fruchtbringende Gesellschaft* mixes dactyls
and iambs, and is plentifully garnished with internal rhymes. The
emblem of the society was a palm tree, in the shape of which, in
accordance with a fashionable conceit, the poem is arranged. The
general effect is not to bother the reader much with details of meaning:

Übliche liebliche
Früchte muß allezeit bringen
Des Palmenbaums ewige Zier,
Darunter auch Fürsten selbst singen,
Lehren und mehren mit heißer Begier
Die Rechte der deutschen hochprächtigen Zungen,
Die sich mit ewigem Preise geschwungen
Hoch über die anderen Sprachen empor:
Wie vor
Dies Land
Mit Hand
Durch Krieg
Durch Sieg,
Durch Fleiß
Mit Schweiß
Den Preis
Das Pfand
Entwandt
Der Welt
Wie aus der Tat erhellt.

The first stanza of a *Maienlied*, dedicated to the Empress Eleonore in
1653, depends largely on the metrical interest provided by a succession
of short dactylic lines:

Glimmert ihr Sterne,
Schimmert von ferne,
Blinkert nicht trübe,
Flinkert zu Liebe
Dieser erfreulichen lieblichen Zeit.
Lachet, ihr Himmel,
Machet Getümmel,
Regnet uns Segen,
Segnet den Regen,
Der uns in Freude verwandelt das Leid.

Negatively, it could be said that language is used here as a 'rhythmic medium without concrete relationships, lacking logical cohesion';[1] positively, that this is poetry over-anxious to show that, if it wants music, it can itself provide it. But though, as some sixteenth-century lyrics in England show, a 'rhythmical tune' can be usefully suggestive to a composer,[2] here the metrical jingle is too insistent to tempt a composer to add more than a tonal veneer. So Meier's setting, Ex. 23 lacking even a good tune, is virtually superfluous.

Both of Zesen's most important collections were published at Hamburg, the *Dichterische Jugend-Flammen* in 1651, and the *Dichterisches Rosen- und Liljentahl* (including the song just quoted) nineteen years later. About half of the twenty-nine melodies in the former were provided by Malachias Siebenhaar, an obscure Magdeburg clergyman whom Zesen held in high regard. Among other contributors were Albert, Meier, and Schop, and the last two contributed also to the more important *Dichterisches Rosen- und Liljentahl*. Occasionally a setting allows itself some freedom of movement and embellishment. Then the result is not ineffective so long as no more is expected Ex. 24 than a decorative interplay of ornate effects. Where the verse itself is acoustically not too ambitious, Siebenhaar can add at least a pleasantly attractive lilt. Ex. 25

With the Nuremberg writers, as with Zesen, it is usual to emphasize the part played in their poetry by dancing metres and onomatopoeia, as in Klaj's *Vorzug des Sommers*:

> Im Lenzen, da glänzen die blümigen Auen,
> Die Auen, die bauen die perlenen Tauen,
> Die Nymphen in Sümpfen ihr Antlitz beschauen,
> Es schmilzet der Schnee,
> Man segelt zur See,
> Bricht güldenen Klee.
> &c.

Their verse tends to have more serious aspects than Zesen's, combining aural virtuosity with themes that command attention, as with Birken's *Spazierlust*:

> Hellglänzendes Silber! mit welchem sich gatten
> Der astigen Linden weitstreifende Schatten!
> Deine sanftkühlend geruhige Lust
> Ist jedem bewußt.

---

[1] P. Hankamer, *Deutsche Gegenreformation und Deutsches Barock*, Stuttgart, 1935, p. 198.
[2] Pattison, op. cit., p. 146.

Wie sollten kunstahmende Pinsel bemalen
Die Blätter, die schirmen vor brennenden Strahlen?
Keiner der Stämme, so grünlich beziert,
Die Ordnung verführt.

Es lispeln und wispeln die schlüpfrigen Brunnen,
Von ihnen ist diese Begrünung gerunnen.
Sie schauren, betrauren und fürchten bereit
Die schneeichte Zeit. . . .

Just as here the ephemerality of living things is delightfully associated with the idyllic impression of nature in high summer, mirrored in a fountain and conveyed in dancing rhythms, in his madrigal poem *An eine Linde* Klaj is not concerned with nature only in so far as it enables him to construct a pattern of interesting sounds:

Schöne Linde!
Deine Rinde
Nehm den Wunsch von meiner Hand:
Kröne mit den sanften Schatten
Diese saatbegrasten Matten,
Stehe sicher vor dem Brand!
Reißt die graue Zeit hier nieder
Deine Brüder;
Soll der Lenz diese Äst
Jedes Jahr belauben wieder
Und dich hegen wurzelfest.

Schottel, in his *Ausführliche Arbeit von der Teutschen Haubt Sprache*, defined the characteristics of the German language in terms of sound, but his argument includes the idea that, freed from corruption, it has it within its power to express divine reality. Provided one does not overlook this serious concern with man and nature, it is not far wide of the mark to describe the poetry of the Nuremberg writers as characterized by an 'orgy of onomatopoeia' and 'dancing figures in sound', as treating poetry as 'an instrument on which to play music',[1] a conception exemplified also in the work of Harsdörffer and finding its culminating expression in the writing of Klaj.

Born in 1607 to a well-to-do Nuremberg family, Philipp Harsdörffer became an official in the town, and was elected to the *Fruchtbringende Gesellschaft*, the *Deutschgesinnte Genossenschaft*, and the *Gekrönte Blumenorden*. He rose to be a member of the city council and died in 1658. From 1641 he published a sort of journal, the *Frauenzimmer*

---

[1] E. Hederer (ed.), *Deutsche Dichtung des Barock*, Munich, n.d., p. 494.

*Gesprechspiele*, incorporating information on all manner of subjects, tucked away among which is the opera *Seelewig*. The question of the sound-effects in Harsdörffer's poetry was examined some years ago by Wolfgang Kayser, who concluded that Harsdörffer was obsessed 'by the feeling that the sound of words has a direct relationship to the processes of nature', but that his aim was not so much the pictorialism of *Klangmalerei*, as the use of tonal equivalents covered by the term *Klangentsprechung*.[1] In either case stress must be placed on his desire to exploit the acoustical properties of poetry, but it was left to Johann Klaj, pushing this tendency to its limits, to render music quite literally superfluous.

Klaj, a friend of Harsdörffer, had been in close touch with Buchner as a student at Wittenberg and, having settled in Nuremberg, collaborated with Harsdörffer in founding the *Gekrönte Blumenorden*. Fellow members included Birken and Staden (composer of *Seelewig*), and also Johann Michael Dilherr, vicar of St. Sebaldus. Klaj was on the staff of the church from 1647, and it was there that his 'oratorios' were heard, among them the *Aufferstehung Jesu Christi* (1644), *Höllen- und Himmelfahrt Jesu Christi* (1644), *Der leidende Christus* (1645), and *Herodes der Kindermörder* (1645). Klaj had discussed Italian monody with Harsdörffer. The text and music of *Seelewig* bear traces of its influence, and it may well have encouraged Klaj to emulate in words effects comparable to those of musical recitative, achieved by a kind of free verse mixing longer and shorter lines. Metrical variety plays an important part in these texts, which, ranging between passages of this kind and dancing dactyls, were declaimed in a half-speaking, half-singing voice. Music, in so far as it played any part, was incidental. The style of performance is indicated in Harsdörffer's proposal, in connexion with *Herodes der Kindermörder*, that short lines should be used for lamentation, as if 'speech were being interrupted by groaning and sighing'.

A position was thus reached opposite to that in which poetry had once been regarded as incomplete without music. Meanwhile German poetry had become more independent by becoming in its way more musical. What Klaj exemplifies is the ultimate and rather absurd possibility along this line of development, a type of literature with an aim tantamount to abrogating the functions of a musical genre.

[1] *Die Klangmalerei bei Harsdörffer*, Leipzig, 1932, p. 54.

# X

## The End of the Continuo Lied

### ANDREAS GRYPHIUS AND CARL FRIEDRICH BRIEGEL

CHRISTIAN WEISE'S remark in 1684, in the preface to Krüger's setting of poems of his in the *Musicalische Ergötzlichkeit*, that all that remained of significance in the lied was survivals 'of fifty years ago', would take us back to the beginning of Albert's career as a song composer, though Weise can hardly have intended to exclude Krieger. Supporting evidence for a pessimistic view at this time is provided by the end, for all practical purposes, of the vigorous tradition in Hamburg with the second edition (1672) of settings by Coler and others in the *Abgewechselte Liebesflammen* of poems by Georg Heinrich Weber, a friend of Rist and a member of the *Elbenschwanenorden*. Chronologically the decay of the lied coincides more or less with the decline of baroque lyrical poetry, though it is difficult to assess the implications of this in terms of cause and effect. Opitz was dead by 1639, Fleming by 1640. Weckherlin, Klaj, Harsdörffer, and Dach all died in the 1650's, Gryphius and Rist in the 1660's, Hofmannswaldau and Paul Gerhardt in the 1670's, and the 1680's saw the death of Zesen, Birken, Neumark, Schirmer, and Homburg. Collections like Morhof's *Teutsche Gedichte* (1682) and Weise's *Reiffe Gedancken* (1683) added nothing of significance.

Poetry had widened its scope by developing musical features of its own, and music in its turn was becoming increasingly interested in more expansive possibilities of expression in less restrictive fields. Opera was luxuriating into more elaborate forms, and, while its own beginnings in Germany had been intimately bound up with the beginnings of the lied, it was growing less and less tolerant of those lied elements which earlier it had had little difficulty in absorbing. It had always been associated with the courts, not only because they alone had the means to foster it, but also because in its magnificence and its themes, taken mainly from mythology, it served to project the ideal of princely power. (Harsdörffer's *Seelewig* had exceptionally what might be called a moral theme, but it was intended for a patrician audience at Nuremberg.) For some time the *Liedoper*, or *Singspiel*, had been the main operatic form, but the latter part of the seventeenth century saw the growing importance of Italian grand opera, with its lavish stage effects and Da capo aria. Princely absolutism, favoured in its development by the settlement after the Thirty Years War, was looking with envious eyes towards the greater pageantry of the French court, and French influence was gaining ground under the stimulus of France's success at the Peace of Westphalia in annexing substantial areas of western Germany. The French overture, created by Lully, established itself in Germany, and in the dotted rhythm of its slow introduction and the brilliance of its faster section affirmed the swagger of an aristocratic way of life.

Even in Hamburg, where extreme simplicity had been a feature of the lied and where also the recently founded opera had a relatively popular basis, the lied, in so far as it still existed, was becoming more elaborate and ornate. In religious song one of the few features of interest in the last twenty years of the century was the collaboration of Johann Wolfgang Franck, who had connexions with the Hamburg opera, with Heinrich Elmenhorst. The latter, a Hamburg clergyman, was a poor poet, though he also published a pastoral comedy, and some opera libretti (two of which Franck set to music). He was as much interested in opera as in the Church, and his *Dramatologia* (1688) defended the Hamburg opera against charges that it was blasphemous and indecorous, stressing its value as a place where the German language was used and where consequently 'good and honourable German customs were bound to prevail'. (Mattheson too emphasized the educational role of the Hamburg opera as 'a university . . . in which architecture, perspective, painting, mechanical skill, dance, oratory, morals, history, poetry, and especially music, are combined in the most pleasing way to unite and uplift a rational audience'.)[1] Elmenhorst provided most of the texts for four collections of songs by Franck between 1681 and 1700. Some are chorale-like settings of these earnest but undistinguished poems, but a tendency towards repetition and coloratura, as in *Jesu neigt sein Haupt und stirbt*, reflects the pressure of changing taste.

Eight years before the foundation of opera in Hamburg, and as the creative period of the baroque lied was virtually over, there were published in 1670, at a small and unimportant German court, settings by a minor composer of poems by the best of all German baroque poets. Here, for the last time in the century, good poetry and good

[1] *Die neueste Untersuchung der Singspiele*, Hamburg, 1744, p. 87.

music meet on equal terms in continuo lieder strictly strophic, but no longer secular.

Briegel received his musical training at Nuremberg, where he was born in 1626. An organist, he took charge of the court's music at Gotha, and was music tutor to the reigning family. His pupils included Elisabeth, daughter of Ernst the Pious. When in 1666 she married Landgraf Ludwig VI of Darmstadt, Briegel followed her and stayed in Darmstadt till his death in 1709. He was a composer of instrumental and religious works, of a ballet-opera, and of incidental music for Gryphius's play *Das verliebte Gespenst*. He evidently had good taste in poetry, judging by the quite important writers represented in his *Geistliche Arien* (1660–1), *Musicalischer Lebens-Brunnen* (1680), and *Letzter Schwanen-Gesang* (1709). These include Gryphius, who, though he was the best of seventeenth-century German poets, was so neglected by song composers that his name does not even figure in the index of Kretzschmar's history of the baroque and eighteenth-century lied.

Gryphius, after all, showed his greatest art in one of the forms, the sonnet, in which baroque poetry most successfully asserted its independence, and within its formal obligations he was able to achieve a remarkable range of expression, from stoic resignation to impassioned desperation, and to develop a wide variety of rhythmic possibilities. His Pindaric Odes, with a similarly exalted tone, were not envisaged as requiring a composer's assistance. The poetry in the *Thränen über das Leiden Jesu Christi* (1652) is much less ambitious, its purpose was purely devotional, and as a matter of convenience the texts were written to familiar tunes, like:

> O grimmge Herzenrisse,
> O herbe Seelenbisse,
> O allzuspäte Reu!
> Was hilft, sich selbst anklagen?
> Was hilft, vor allen sagen
> Von gar zu hart verletzter Treu?

—to *O Welt, ich muß dich lassen*, by this time a well-known religious adaptation of *Innsbruck ich muß dich lassen*. Gryphius's poetry in this style, straightforward in thought, language, and rhythm, invites musical setting especially in the chorale tradition, and this may well have been in his mind when he wrote it.

Ex. 26    Briegel's *Geistliche Oden Andreae Gryphii* is the only set of baroque lieder, with the possible exception of Fleming's poetry in Pohle's

*Zwölf Liebesgesänge*, that might be regarded as a song-cycle. Pohle was a musician at several courts with close family and geographical connexions with Elector Georg I of Saxony, and his settings are interesting for their mixture of styles. About half of them are strophic lieder with ritornelli, and the remainder are through-composed and make considerable use of pictorialism and coloratura, which links them to cantata—not so much perhaps of the more operatic kind as that represented by Schütz's *Kleine geistliche Konzerte*. But it could be argued that the only unity of the *Zwölf Liebesgesänge* is a sequence of texts by a single poet on the same general theme. Briegel's texts, however, incorporating also two poems by Gryphius's son, Christian, are so arranged as to give the work features of a genuine song-cycle. Its unity is built around the theme of the 'peace of the spirit', the title of the seventh song. This is preceded by a series of tormented meditations on the ephemerality of life and is followed with moving effect by supplications to God and meditation on the promise of grace. After two intervening numbers, in which human nothingness can now be faced with assured belief, the cycle concludes with a song of serene farewell to the world.

Earlier, as in the *Geistlicher Musicalischer Rosen-garten*, Briegel had used sequences, word-painting, repetition, and coloratura to interpret his texts, and the *Evangelische Gespräche* (1660–81) have dramatically expressive sections reminiscent of Monteverdi's *Lamento d'Arianne*. But in Darmstadt, where he was concerned about the low state of the church music, his immediate concern was to make people more interested in it, and in the *Evangelisches Hosianna* (from 1677) he explains that he had therefore decided that it would be helpful if he provided music related to the gospel story, with or without instruments, and above all easy to perform. He had therefore asked a clergyman, Johann Samuel Kriegsmann, to prepare suitable texts, and Kriegsmann had made these as simple as he could. Briegel made the music easy too, so that the gospel story might be heard in places where people could only sing a simple tune. In the *Musicalische Trostquelle* (1679) and the *Evangelisches Hosianna* (which reached a second edition in 1690) chorales are so arranged that the lower parts could, if necessary, be taken over by the continuo. In such works Briegel's aims were comparable to Rist's, whose influence may be suspected also in the Gryphius settings.

Each piece in the *Geistliche Oden Andreae Gryphii* has a short introduction for two violins, and the use of the scordatura is presumably intended to make it the easier to play. It always has some rhythmic relationship to the song that follows, and it can be repeated between the verses, but nothing much is lost if it is omitted altogether, except in the case of No. 3, where the voice 'concerts' with the instruments in a very simple way. This may be only to vary the role of the strings for the performers' interest, but the instruments participate in the pleasing effect whereby the drooping appoggiatura figure in the upper parts contrasts with the stolid bass built on a conventional formula of chords, whose roots rise a fourth. No. 10 alone is for two voices, possibly to give the person for whom the songs were intended the chance to sing a duet with a friend. In general, melismatic figures and awkward or unexpected intervals are avoided, and the melody, aided by an eloquent use of rests, always follows the shape of the poetic line easily and naturally. The florid decoration in the instrumental parts of No. 2, which has declamatory features unusual in the baroque lied, and also in No. 6, is less typical than the chorale-like melody of Nos. 1 and 11. The dotted rhythm in No. 8 is effective, so too is Briegel's ability, here and elsewhere, to combine tunefulness with features eloquently embodying something of the expressive liberties of recitative. The harmony is not particularly exciting, but has interesting features, as sometimes at the cadences. No. 4 is particularly attractive, transmitting the sombreness of the theme by the lightest of dancing melodies. As if rendering the thought of transience more tolerable by making a game with death, it dances serenely to its close at the words *Der Erden sagen Gute Nacht*.

# PART III

<code>⫷⫸ ⫷⫸ ⫷⫸ ⫷⫸ ⫷⫸ ⫷⫸ ⫷⫸ ⫷⫸ ⫷⫸ ⫷⫸ ⫷⫸</code>

## XI

## Aria and Song in the Later Baroque

### PHILIPP ERLEBACH

HAMBURG had no court, but it enjoyed the material advantages of
a flourishing commercial centre. Its prosperous middle-class was
dominated by a minority of well-to-do and influential patricians, and,
like all the larger towns in seventeenth-century Germany, its administration was oligarchical. Opera, established there in 1678, opened
with a *Singspiel* by Theile, and works of this kind, in the *Liedoper*
tradition, were characteristic of Strungk and Franck in the early
phase. Kusser brought with him from Wolfenbüttel a conception
of opera combining French and Italian features, but ingredients like
the Da capo aria and French overture coexist in his work with dance-
airs and melodious duets that 'bespeak French influence as clearly
as strophic songs do that of the popular German *Singspiel*'.[1] Even
with Keiser, whom Steffani held in high esteem and whose conception of opera tended towards artistic and financial extravagance,
one finds a catchy tunefulness, borrowed from the *Liedoper*.

There is an obvious link here with the continuo lied, and selections
of songs of this kind from the operas towards the end of the century
to some extent satisfied needs that this might otherwise have provided.
But in other respects opera was increasingly conditioning taste in
the direction of the musically more ambitious aria—the term, earlier
synonymous with lied, now coming to denote the Da capo form.
Mattheson, who was associated with the Hamburg opera, decided by
1722, in the *Critica Musica*,[2] that the strophic lied was intolerably
dull. French instrumental music too, which for some time had influenced the baroque lied in particular respects, was now attracting
special attention. The *Parodies bacchiques*, first published in 1695 and

[1] Bukofzer, op. cit., p. 309.          [2] i. 100.

so called because the tunes originally had other texts or had been composed for instruments, was widely influential, as when Gaspari, a Leipzig dancing-master, in 1713 published his *Texte auf die gebräuchlichsten Tänze*. In Leipzig there is a manuscript collection of songs copied in 1719 under the title *Musikalische Rüstkammer*, 'consisting of all kinds of beautiful and jolly airs, minuets, sarabands, gigues and marches', in which, illustrating the distortions often resulting from this practice, the words, with a trifling change or two, of Krieger's Ex. 27 *Ihr schönen Augen* are attached to the tune of a minuet. This is quite different from what happened earlier when Hammerschmidt in his Ex. 28 *Weltliche Oden* set a well-known poem of Fleming's as a gavotte of the kind common in French dance-suites. Here the words fit the tune so naturally that the gavotte rhythm must surely have influenced the poem.

The oligarchic character of a town like Hamburg facilitated the adoption of a courtly form like opera, but in a predominantly bourgeois setting this could hardly flourish without modification. The baroque opera in Hamburg, a mixture of the lavish *opera seria* with features of *opera buffa*, utilized local subjects, allowed songs in dialect, and rejected castrati. It was the child of a transitional situation, the baroque era beginning now to shade over into the Enlightenment, and its social setting had features of its own. Mattheson, in *Die neueste Untersuchung der Singspiele*, insisted on the more refined aspects when he said that it would be absurd if 'everything happened as crudely on the stage as on the market-place', for 'operas demand something quite different, something more extraordinary. Even in the most ordinary speech it must contain nothing . . . associated with the mob, or vulgarly natural.'[1] The aim of opera, however, is not merely to arouse pleasure, he explained in *Der moralische Patriot* (1728); it 'is important that virtue should be praised and vice dishonoured'.[2] Emphasis on the moral aspect, not a characteristic feature of courtly opera, characterizes the attitude of the Hamburg opera librettist, Barthold Feind, who in his *Gedancken von der Opera* defends the Da capo aria on condition that it is linked with a moral message.

This combination of interest in operatic forms and moral themes defines the angle from which to approach the last collection of secular ('political') lieder published in Germany in the seventeenth century, Erlebach's *Harmonische Freude musicalischer Freunde*, with texts attributed to Christian Helm, an official of the Rudolstadt court.

[1] p. 80.      [2] p. 118.

The first part, 'consisting of fifty moral and political arias, with ritornelli, with two violins and continuo', was published at Nuremberg in 1697. A second part appeared in 1710, by which time Erlebach had issued a collection of twelve religious pieces, *Die Gott-geheiligte Sing-Stunde*. His remark that 'distinguished friends' had pressed him to compose religious songs might associate the change with the lowered prestige of the secular lied, while the sub-title, offering possibilities of performance with chorus and instruments, could suggest a desire to work at something more ambitious. Certainly the second part of the *Harmonische Freude* is more elaborate, even operatic, in places. Recitative occurs in No. 3, and, by the previous standards of the German continuo lied, No. 15, for example, is quite extravagant. Also the instruments called for are more numerous and varied. The use of a string quartet is common, and one song requires three oboes and a bassoon.

The reigning house at Rudolstadt was that of Schwarzburg-Holstein, a pious Protestant family interested in good works, and paternalistically benevolent towards its subjects. The first ruler under whom Erlebach served was Albert Anton (1641–1710), who was widely esteemed and in due course promoted to the rank of *Reichsfürst*. His sister, Ludämilie Elisabeth, who died in 1672 and whom Printz praises in the *Historische Beschreibung* for her 'admirably clever verse', has a corner in German literature through her religious poems, published posthumously in 1687 as *Die Stimme der Freundin* and described in the sub-title as 'Geistliche Lieder . . . aus brünstiger und bis ans Ende beharreter Jesus-Liebe'. His wife, Ämalia Juliane, was no less pious, and also a prolific versifier. Her *Geistliche Lieder und Gebete vor und nach Erlangung des göttlichen Ehesegens* appeared in 1683, followed in 1685 by her *Kühlwasser in großer Hitze des Creutzes*. These ladies were in close touch with Ahasver Fritsch, who went to Rudolstadt in 1657 as tutor to the reigning family and stayed on to become a prominent figure in the administration, writing in his spare time poetry with fervently pious titles, like *Neue Himmelsüße Jesus-Lieder* (1668) and *Himmels-Lust und Welt-Unlust* (1670). With the accession of Ludwig Friedrich in 1710 a more worldly tone began to be felt at court, and from 1729 until 1754, sixteen years after the Hamburg opera had closed, baroque opera found a home at Rudolstadt, though elsewhere its day was over or passing. However, before this there is evidence of theatrical activities in the group of stage-works, dating mainly from the 1660's, probably (though only the texts survive) of the *Liedoper* variety, which were written for domestic cele-brations in the ruling house. *Die erfreuete Unschuld*, performed in 1666, was the last of them, until in 1680 *Die Steigende und fallende Athenia oder Eudoxia* was commissioned for a birthday in the reigning family.

By this time Erlebach had been only a year at Rudolstadt, and it was not until nearer the turn of the century that theatre music, mainly serenades and ballets, showed more definite signs of establishing itself there. The extent of Erlebach's participation is unclear. He certainly wrote opera, and his *Die Plejades oder das Siebengestirn* was performed at Brunswick. Gottsched (in the *Nöthiger Vorrat zur Geschichte der deutschen dramatischen Dichtkunst*) mentions an opera performed at Rudolstadt in 1686, and in Freiesleben's *Nachlese zu Gottscheds nöthigem Vorrat* there is a reference under Erlebach's name to the *Streit der Fama*. The death of Ämalia Juliane in 1706 caused an interruption of theatrical activities, leaving only a short interval before Erlebach died in 1714. By this time he had had Lully's works added to the court's music library, and probably too the volume of *Allerhand Teutsche Opern wie auch italienische Teutsche Arien*, which was on the shelves from about 1700.

Erlebach's compositions include some of the most important forms of the seventeenth century, instrumental works in the French style, Passion music, and cantatas, and his songs have considerable variety. Some of these have rather an instrumental character, influenced by French dance-rhythms, and occasionally, as can easily be illustrated, Ex. 29 the verse seems even to have been fitted to a particular type of tune. Between simpler pieces of this kind and arias elaborate enough to be more or less cantatas, there are a number of impressive songs which, while considerably affective, are still basically strophic in conception, though no longer continuo lieder in the simplest sense. One example would be *Meine Seufzer, meine Klagen* (I. 14), apropos of which Spitta, talking about Bach's power to express grief, remarks that only Erlebach 'had composed anything approaching this'. In the same context he surmises, on slender evidence, that Bach 'may quite well have known Erlebach's collection of arias'.[1] (Pirro too speaks of the *Harmonische Freude* as 'a collection of airs that Bach doubtless was familiar with from his youth',[2] but his comparison of certain motifs only proves that both composers sometimes used similar devices.) Another example is the setting of the text on the opposite page:

[1] *J. S. Bach*, London, 1899, i. 351.
[2] *L'Esthétique de J. S. Bach*, Paris, 1907, p. 45.

Kommt, ihr Stunden, macht mich frei
Von des Lebens Tyrannei.
Glaubt, ich weiß mich nicht zu fassen,
Meine Qual ist allzu groß;
Ich steh aller Hoffnung los
Ganz verlassen.
Kommt, ihr Stunden, macht mich frei
Von des Lebens Tyrannei.

Selbst die Freunde stellen sich,
Wenn ich klage, wider mich.
Sie verlachen mein Verderben,
Meine Pein mehrt ihren Scherz;
Will mein abgezehrtes Herz
Gleich ersterben.
Selbst die Freunde stellen sich,
Wenn ich klage, wider mich.

Was mein Leben sonst erfreut,
Bringt mir jetzo Traurigkeit,
Wo ich vormals Lust gefunden,
Fühl ich jetzt nur Weh und Ach,
Darum meiner Tränen Bach
Alle Stunden.
Was mein Leben sonst erfreut,
Bringt mir jetzo Traurigkeit.

Hört der Himmel denn doch nicht,
Was mein Hertze klagend spricht?
Klipp und Felsen, Flut und Wellen,
Drohen mir Gefahr und Not;
Ach mein schwankes Hoffnungsboot
Will zerschellen.
Hört der Himmel denn doch nicht,
Was mein Hertze klagend spricht?

Ach, ihr Stunden, macht mich los,
Mein Verhängnis ist zu groß.
Laßt mich bald das Ufer küssen,
Jammerwelt, dir sag ich auf.
Himmel, du wirst meinen Lauf
Glücklich schließen!
Ach, ihr Stunden, macht mich los,
Mein Verhängnis ist zu groß.

Though the music is *con affetto*, the text is exceedingly dull. Tired Ex. 30
resignation, coupled with longing for death and anticipation of heavenly
bliss, is its theme, banal lines with cliché rhymes succeeding each

other like a mechanical exercise in the art of anticlimax. Lines more
dead than:

> Glaubt, ich weiß mich nicht zu fassen,
> Meine Qual ist allzu groß,

could hardly be imagined, and their flatulent emotion in a chain of
monosyllables is made the more noticeable by the more or less pretentious stanza form. But they are much more effective in the music; for
example, *Qual* is given prominence through repetition and association
with stressed beats with sometimes longer note-values. In bar 16,
again, Erlebach breaks the mechanical character of the line-units by
passing quickly over the heavy and dull ending of the second of these
lines (*groß*), which, though falling on the first beat of the bar, is relieved
by the stress put on the first syllable of *meine*. Repetition introduces
variety into the jingle of the metre, the same word occurring with
different stress and altered note-values. In the text the clumsy prominence of *groß* is made the more marked by rhyming with an equally
unattractive word in the next line, but this weakness is corrected in
the setting, the stressed *los* being put to a short, unaccented note, as
the music moves to its cadence on *verlassen*. Although a short and
lifeless line in the text, it gives the composer, with the help of embellishment, the opportunity to extend it into a telling dramatic climax.

In this excellent song, a Da capo setting with some coloratura, the
music serves a succession of stanzas, but it accepts only impatiently
the limits of the strophic lied, and its form makes it less lied than
aria. Performed in its entirety, it would support the argument that
the repetitiveness of the strophic lied and the way a Da capo aria
elaborates its textual material are ultimately incompatible. A paradox
of the Da capo aria is that, while it provides more extensive resources
of musical expression, the composer is best served by a text that says
little rather than much and in a way sufficiently commonplace not
to attract or demand too much attention in its own right. This would
make it more than a coincidence that the strophic lied was being
superseded by the aria at a time when, though the German baroque
lyric had always had more than its fair share of banality, its dominant tendency was firmly set in that direction. One cannot therefore
safely say that Erlebach was handicapped by his poor texts, their
drabness aggravated by trite and sententious moralism. The contrary
is more likely to be the case. The more an aria strained to unfold all
its musical possibilities, the more convenient it was if the text did no
more than provide an *Affekt*, and there were even those who inclined

to the view that a simple and uncomplicated *Affekt* was the ideal. The fact that Walther, in his article on aria in the *Musikalisches Lexikon* of 1732, recognized it as a danger inherent in aria that in the interest of musical effect composers sometimes took liberties unjustified by the text, is seen in his advice to composers not to repeat single words unnecessarily, 'especially where they carry no special emphasis'. He thought it, however, preferable to the 'once more usual' strophic song, because amongst other things it prevented the absurdities that arise when reference to laughter in one verse goes to the same music as one to weeping in another.

Remarking that strophic song 'has had to give way . . . to the present type of aria', Walther remembered it not least for its weaknesses, and, in fact, its successes were now more and more forgotten. He speaks quite well of Albert, but he is briefer and more casual about Krieger, of whose earlier popularity and importance one would get no inkling from the *Lexikon*. Strophic song, it is true, was soon to return to prominence, but on the basis of a new type of poetry in association with a different conception of music. Already by the time Walther's *Lexikon* appeared, and within only a few years of the death of Erlebach, the first significant indications of the changing course of German poetry were evident in the work of Brockes which, catching the attention of Handel, provided the texts for the last important set of German continuo lieder in the baroque era—important, that is to say, for their intrinsic value and also for the conflict of style and outlook between music still fully baroque and poetry that could no longer be so described.

# XII

## The Last Phase

### BARTHOLD HEINRICH BROCKES
### AND GEORGE FREDERICK HANDEL

BROCKES was born in Hamburg in 1680 and died there in 1747, twelve years before Handel and three years before Bach. He was a member of the senate and a prominent figure in the public life of the city. His first work (*Serenaden zum Petrimahle*, 1709–10) has a late-baroque extravagance, so too has his Passion text (*Der für die Sünden der Welt gemartete und sterbende Jesus*, 1712), which was used by Bach, Handel, and Telemann, and the same is true of his translation of Marino, published in 1715. A few years later, however, there began to appear, in 1721, a work with quite different characteristics, *Irdisches Vergnügen in Gott*, a long contemplation of nature in blank verse, with lyrical sections interposed. It is from these that Handel took the words of his *Neun Deutsche Arien*, his last work with a German text. The edition referred to in this chapter is that by Hermann Roth, published by Breitkopf & Härtel in 1931.

The composition of the *Neun Deutsche Arien*, published in 1729, was attributed originally by Chrysander to the time of Handel's sojourn in Hannover in 1712, but meanwhile Max Seiffert[1] has shown this to be incorrect. In 1729, three years after his British naturalization, Handel set off for Italy in search of singers for his London operas. On the way back, passing through Germany, he called in at Hamburg, where his first opera had been produced twenty-four years before, and where now his attention was drawn to the *Irdisches Vergnügen in Gott*. Within a few years of setting parts of this to music, Handel turned away from opera, with its courtly associations and its castrati, to oratorio. The revised version of *Esther* (1732) was his first step in this direction. Practical considerations too played a part, like the success in 1728 of *The Beggar's Opera*, and in any case it was not until 1741 that he wrote his last *opera seria*.

The lyrical sections in the *Irdisches Vergnügen in Gott* may well

---

[1] 'Händels deutsche Gesänge', *Liliencron-Festschrift*, Leipzig, 1910.

have been included to attract composers, for, before the whole work had appeared, selections were published under the title *Harmonische Himmels-Lust im Irdischen*, and the sub-title speaks of 'musical poems and cantatas', arranged according to the four seasons. In the foreword Brockes's son mentions that parts of the *Irdisches Vergnügen in Gott* had been set to music without his father's prior knowledge (which does not mean without his approval), and, in addition to two unimportant composers, he refers to Telemann and Handel. He names four of the *Neun Deutsche Arien*, unaware, apparently, that Handel had used five more texts, to which he refers without mentioning Handel. People, he says, who revere 'the power and wisdom of our beneficent Creator' will find here the same ideas as in the *Irdisches Vergnügen in Gott*, 'except that in this collection my father has been concerned not so much with mere contemplation of the beauties of this world, but mainly with those that can give us even greater delight with the help of the divine art of music'. His intention was 'to provide this noble art with material through which its sweet charms can edify the human race'.

The edifying intention of the following poem, one of the texts of the *Neun Deutsche Arien*, is obvious enough:

> Das zitternde Glänzen der spielenden Wellen
> Versilbert das Ufer, beperlet den Strand,
> Die rauschenden Flüsse, die sprudelnden Quellen
> Bereichern, befruchten, erfrischen das Land,
> Und machen in tausend vergnügenden Fällen
> Die Güte des herrlichen Schöpfers bekannt.

But only the last two lines reveal that the poet is describing the beauties of nature only to point the moral that they demonstrate the kindliness of God, and in any case the theological point does not make nature here unimportant, even though Brockes may not have expressed his love for it entirely without ornamental effects. Nature, that is to say, has more than metaphorical significance. *Das zitternde Glänzen, die spielenden Wellen*, may be decoration, but they are also descriptive terms springing from genuine experience. Nor, as commonly in German baroque poetry, is there any tension here between the temporal and the eternal. The language, without the convolutions and complicated imagery of much baroque verse, is 'gentle and sweet'— in the words of Christoph Friedrich Weichmann, to whom Brockes had entrusted the task of seeing the first instalment through the press, and who added a foreword in the second edition.

Such phraseology is also typical of the vocabulary used by eighteenth-century writers to denote the 'galant' music of the post-baroque. While in literature 'galant' had by Gottsched's time come to signify poor taste and excess, in music it signified a style contrasting with anything strained and 'learned', freedom from counterpoint, interest centred on a relaxed, flowing, and 'natural' melody: 'The tune, its direction and its punctuation are all that matters. The gentler Allegros and Allegrettos must float, not scurry; the Graves and Adagios must be urbanely yet unashamedly emotional; and the finale must run, not scramble in the suffocating rush for the exit.'[1] Quantz, taking stock in his *Versuch einer Anweisung die Flöte traversière zu spielen* (1752) of German music 'in the last century or more', says that, lacking good taste, Germans had achieved little in the way of 'beautiful melodies'. Composers 'gave the singers many words to sing one after another in a rapid series of notes, which is incompatible with the quality of good singing, prevents the singer from producing the sounds in their proper beauty, and is too far removed from ordinary speech'.[2]

The change of attitude is seen also in Mattheson's comparison in *Der vollkommene Capellmeister* (Hamburg, 1739)[3] of two poems of his own invention. The first runs:

> Wesen, das nicht nur die Zeiten
> Und die Ewigkeit erfüllet;
> Nein, aus des Vollkommenheiten
> Selbst das Meer der Ewigkeiten
> Wie ein kleines Bächlein quillet;
> Und des Größe doch nur Güte:
> Dich verehret mein Gemüte.

In the second he imagines a person sitting by the bank of a stream and expressing his feelings thus:

> Klarer Spiegel meines Leidens
>     Nimm auch meine Zähren an.
> Laß die lispelnden Crystallen
> Sanfte, sanfte niederfallen!
> Daß zu deinen Silber-Wellen
> Sich mein Tränen-Tau gesellen,
>     Und zu Perlen werden kann.

The several statements in the first example virtually constitute a single sentence, which 'has the appearance of a richly embellished cloak

---

[1] T. Dart, *The Interpretation of Music*, London, 1954, p. 96.
[2] Ed. Schering, Leipzig, 1906, pp. 254–5.                          [3] 9. Hauptstück.

because of its length and complexity', its *viele Distinctionen*. It is not, Mattheson thinks, a 'musical' poem, because its melody could not rest until the end. Though it is longer than the first, the second example comprises three 'periods' forming a single 'paragraph'. It would therefore, in contrast to the strained continuity of the former, give the music intermediary points of repose. It is more 'flowing', and therefore more 'singable'. A further reason why the reader would accept the first example as characteristic of some baroque poetry is that it contrasts the puny world of human effort with the infinite and eternal, and this accounts for its strained syntax. The second poem stands aside from these weighty matters and contemplates man in idyllic unity with nature. Mattheson's remark in the *Critica Musica* about the virtues of the poetry of Neukirch and König is based on similar criteria: 'Such sweet, flowing, pleasing, concise phrases, with their short periods, which are so easy to set to music and to sing, must be regarded as an essentially musical feature of poetry. Thus it is with the works of König and Neukirch, both of whom give the composer just what he wants, so that it is sheer joy to write music to their texts.'[1] Elsewhere in the *Critica Musica* Mattheson expresses the same idea by saying that 'concise sentences and statements are musical, but not drawn-out and incapsulated periods':

Kurzgefaßte Sätze (*propositiones*) und Sprüche (*sententiae*) gehören zur Musik; keine weitläufige und in einander geschränkte *periodi*. . . .[2]

By this standard a musical text would be one in which, above all, the melody has opportunities naturally to come to rest at points before the close. This incidentally would apply to all the poetry of the kind that had been favoured by the baroque lied composers, and, equally significantly, it would be conspicuously untrue of the type that they had neglected. By this standard a poem, like the following by Lohenstein, would be judged unmusical:

Narziß, der seinen Durst allhier zu löschen meinte,
Geriet, in sich verliebt, durch diesen Quell in Glut,
Durch Kält und Brand ins Grab. Alleine diese Flut,
Die ihm zum Sterben half, doch bald den Tod beweinte,
Bezeugt, wie sehr sie ihn des Lebens schätzet wert,
Weil sie die Blumen netzt, in die er ward verkehrt

—and, by an equivalent standard in music, Quantz could have been expected to criticize Handel's melodic line in his setting of *Das zitternde* Ex. 31

[1] i. 101.          [2] ii. 300.

*Glänzen der spielenden Wellen*, which he would have thought too far removed from what is natural to the voice, too lacking in cantabile qualities, and, above all, too hurried and restless. He would also have said that it strove too much after effect, for, while the melismatic treatment, for example, of *spielende Wellen* is, from one point of view, conventional word-painting, from another, since the element of decoration predominates, it adds an ornamental feature to Brockes's directer experience of nature.

The text here culminates in the point that the beauties of nature testify to the goodness of God, and they are described to establish this conclusion. But in this Da capo aria the words:

> Und machen in tausend vergnügenden Fällen
> Die Güte des herrlichen Schöpfers bekannt,

constitute, not the conclusion, but a passing episode. The setting takes the poem back to its beginning, and it ends at *beperlet den Strand.* Ex. 32 The same thing happens in the fourth of the *Neun Deutsche Arien*:

> Süße Stille, sanfte Quelle
> Ruhiger Gelassenheit!
> Selbst die Seele wird erfreut,
> Wenn ich mir nach dieser Zeit
> Arbeitsamer Eitelkeit
> Jene Ruh vor Augen stelle,
> Die uns ewig ist bereit,

where, after the reference to 'jene Ruh . . . die uns ewig ist bereit', which is the climax of the poem, the music returns to the peace of nature. The emphasis is even more altered in this case because, whereas in the poem only two lines are devoted to the description of nature and five to theological considerations, in the song roughly the same number of bars is given to the opening two lines as to the remaining five. This weights the emphasis heavily on the theme of nature's *süße Stille*, even without taking account of the repeat. This would be all the more striking if it were agreed that, as in the preceding example, the vocal line is least interesting in its middle section.

In the first part, and its repeat, the music adds more ornate qualities than the verse possesses, particularly bearing in mind the additional effects that at the reprise improvised embellishment should add to Handel's written notes. It imposes a significant degree of sophistication upon the easy, not to say naïve, serenity of Brockes's contentment, significant because the sophistication makes the relation between nature's peace and the experience of it remoter. The first appearance of *süße Stille* is to a gentle, flowing phrase, gracefully embellished on the second syllable of *süße*, comfortably placed for the voice, communicated therefore without a sense of strain, and accepted by the listener as an expression of peace. Its second appearance is to an equally relaxed and relaxing phrase—again ornamented, this time on the first syllable of *süße*—with the serenest interval possible in the drop of an octave. But there is a suggestion of agitation in the dotted rhythm of the ornamental figure. When the vocal line, rising to the first syllable of the *sanfte*, falls gently at *ruhiger*, the voice, instead of accepting the mood of Brockes's verse and lingering on the repose of the cadence on the last syllable of *ruhiger*, hurries impetuously forward on a rising melismatic figure, excitement replacing serenity and disturbing Brockes's acceptance of peace calmly enjoyed. When *süße Stille* makes its third appearance, it is to a suddenly rising phrase, as if the voice were reaching out for peace, entreating it rather than participating in it. The added sixth at *sanfte* is only a mild dissonance, and the treble and bass lead one to expect it, but, occurring on the stressed syllable of this particular word, is worth noticing. Again the voice falls to a cadence, at *ruhiger Gelassenheit*, but, in the ensuing bars when it is silent, the intrusion of the flattened leading note at least does not wholly confirm the mood of peace. The voice has one further gesture to make. It repeats *ruhiger Gelassenheit*, but with effort and supplication implied by the high phrase on *ruhiger*, before at *Gelassenheit* it repeats the dying fall.

If Brockes's theme of nature's peace comes through rather differently in the song than in the poem, what of the other aspect, the peace of God that through his experience of nature Brockes so confidently assumes? The relevant part of the song begins at the third bar of the second section, where the voice has a strained and angular phrase at the beginning of *selbst die Seele wird erfreut*. A few bars later the same thing happens at the crucial reference to *jene Ruh*, and with the additional and telling feature that the interval is then immediately repeated. Confident possession of *jene Ruh* is hardly affirmed in music such as this, which means that Chrysander's description of these songs as 'full of contentment . . . carefree and at peace with God'[1] requires at least a little modification.

Brockes closes the gap between man and God, not by adjusting human values to the 'deserts of vast eternity' that turn honour to dust

---

[1] *G. F. Händel*, i, 1858, p. 373.

and lust to ashes, but by a conception of nature quite different from that characteristic of the baroque. He can identify himself with nature and thereby anticipate the peace of God. The sense of Handel's music, however, is that, much though he may desire it, a union as idyllic as this is in the last resort at least not without its difficulties. His song, in Girdlestone's phrase[1] about Rameau's pastoral music, is 'too intense for true calm', leaving behind a 'feeling of disturbance, not of peace'. Above all, it dramatizes Brockes's theme of peace, and, if an idyll at all, it is an idyll in the grand style, with theatrical gesture, a 'heroic idyll'.[2]

In the transition, now to be considered, of the lied from the baroque the peace of nature will not be an object of supplication, as with Handel, nor will it require Brockes's theological references. It will be imagined as possible amid an idealized nature, and in pastoral guise the poet will escape from courtly artificiality and in idyllic seclusion, by woods and streams, will playfully live the dream of happiness and peace, of the perfection attainable by bourgeois man freed from his own forms of corruption. The typical features of the early and mid-eighteenth century—the idea of the 'best of all possible worlds', deism, the optimistic belief in a harmonious order of things, and the notion of happiness as the goal of life—unite in the post-baroque lied, expressing the aspirations of the rising bourgeoisie to free itself from feudality, without yet thinking in terms of power.

[1] *Jean-Philippe Rameau*, London, 1957, pp. 387, 388.
[2] E. Bücken, *Die Musik des Rokokos und der Klassik*, Wildpark-Potsdam, 1927, p. 71.

# XIII

## *The Transition*

FRIEDRICH VON HAGEDORN, GEORG PHILIPP TELEMANN
AND JOHANN VALENTIN GÖRNER

IN *Die Welt*, one of Hofmannswaldau's best-known poems, he contrasts in characteristically baroque manner the nothingness and transience of worldly things with the permanence and splendour of divine reality:

> Was ist die Welt und ihr berühmtes Glänzen?
> Was ist die Welt und ihre ganze Pracht?
> Ein schnöder Schein in kurzgefaßten Grenzen,
> Ein schneller Blitz bei schwarzgewölkter Nacht;
> Ein buntes Feld, da Kummerdisteln grünen,
> Ein schön Spital, so voller Krankheit steckt;
> Ein Sklavenhaus, da alle Menschen dienen,
> Ein faules Grab, so Alabaster deckt.
> Das ist der Grund, darauf wir Menschen bauen,
> Und was das Fleisch für einen Abgott hält.
> Komm, Seele, komm und lerne weiter schauen,
> Als sich erstreckt der Zirkel dieser Welt.
> Streich ab von dir derselben kurzes Prangen,
> Halt ihre Lust für eine schwere Last.
> So wirst du leicht in diesen Port gelangen,
> Da Ewigkeit und Schönheit sich umfaßt.

Hagedorn, whose *Oden und Lieder* makes him one of the most significant post-baroque poets of the first half of the eighteenth century, expressed his criticism of this ornate and metaphorical kind of verse in a poem addressed to Hofmannswaldau:

> Zum Dichter machten dich die Lieb' und die Natur.
> O wärst du dieser stets, wie Opitz, treu gewesen!
> Du würdest noch mit Ruhm gelesen:
> Jetzt kennt man deinen Schwulst und deine Fehler nur.
> Hat sonst dein Reiz auch Lehrer oft verführet,
> So wirst du jetzt von Schülern kaum berühret.
> Allein, wie viele sind von denen, die dich schmähn,
> Zu metaphysisch schwach, wie du, sich zu vergehn!

H

This is similar to Scheibe's remark that Bach would have done better not to 'allow bombastic and confusing elements (*ein schwülstiges und verworrenes Wesen*) to keep nature out of his art',[1] which is a criticism of what, in his *Dissertation on the Rise, Union and Power of Poetry and Music* (1763), John Brown calls 'the obscure, the learned, the cold, the florid, the wordy, the amusing Style'.[2] Scheibe was a disciple of Gottsched, whose *Versuch einer Critischen Dichtkunst vor die Deutschen* (1730) was influential in its 'enlightened' insistence on good taste based on the imitation of nature, Quantz's verdict on baroque music in the *Versuch einer Anleitung die Flöte traversière zu spielen* (1752) followed similar standards, and he, like Gottsched, was under the influence of the rationalistic philosophy of Wolff.

Hagedorn's own treatment of a theme closely comparable to Hof-mannswaldau's can be studied in a poem with a similar title, *Der Lauf der Welt*:

> Unzählich ist der Schmeichler Haufen,
> Die jeden Großen überlaufen,
> So lang er sich erhält.
> Doch gleitet er von seinen Höhen;
> So kann er bald sich einsam sehen.
> Das ist der Lauf der Welt.
>
> Ein Dürftiger sucht seine Freunde:
> Doch alle meiden ihn als Feinde;
> Allein er erbet Geld.
> Sogleich erscheinen zehn Bekannten
> Und zehn entbehrliche Verwandten.
> Das ist der Lauf der Welt.
>
> Ein Schulfuchs hofft mit dürren Gründen
> Den Beifall aller Welt zu finden:
> Allein er wird geprellt.
> Mein Mädchen macht oft falsche Schlüsse:
> Doch überzeugt sie mich durch Küsse.
> Das ist der Lauf der Welt.
>
> Ein freies Weib von zwanzig Jahren
> Ist zwar in vielem unerfahren:
> Doch, was sie sagt, gefällt.
> Gebt ihr noch zwanzig Jahre drüber:
> So hört man ihre Tochter lieber.
> Das ist der Lauf der Welt.
>
> Leander stimmet süße Töne,
> Und singt und seufzet seiner Schöne,
> Bis ihr das Ohr fast gellt.

---

[1] *Critischer Musicus*, 6. Stück, 14 May 1737.          [2] p. 225.

Allein, eh' er recht ausgesungen,
Hat schon ein andrer sie bezwungen.
Das ist der Lauf der Welt.

Stax sucht am Montag Doris Küsse:
Am Dienstag find't er Hindernisse:
Am Mittwoch siegt der Held.
Am Donnerstag vergehn die Triebe:
Am Freitag sucht er neue Liebe.
Das ist der Lauf der Welt.

Cephise schwört: Sie will ihr Leben
Der stillen Einsamkeit ergeben,
Und höhnt was sich gesellt.
Drauf will sie sich durch Heirat adeln,
Und spricht zu allen, die sie tadeln:
Das ist der Lauf der Welt.

Ein Mädchen voller Weisheitsgründe
Hält jeden Kuß für eine Sünde,
Bis ihr ein Freund gefällt.
Hat dieser sie dann überwunden,
So sagt sie selbst in frohen Stunden:
Das ist der Lauf der Welt.

Wenn junge Witwen traurig scheinen,
Und in dem Mann sich selbst beweinen,
So ist es unverstellt.
Doch keine sieht den Trauerschleier
Mit größrer Lust, als einen Freier.
Das ist der Lauf der Welt.

This poem strikes a more homely note than Hofmannswaldau's, which is not to say that it is a better one. Hofmannswaldau is obsessed with the awe-inspiring solemnity of his theme, but in a more carefree manner Hagedorn reduces his to a series of light-hearted episodes. Hofmannswaldau's poem moves from metaphor to metaphor towards its affirmation of eternity, extending the dimensions of space and time as it proceeds, while Hagedorn's remains close to nature, conceived in simple and idyllic terms, and narrowly confined.

Hagedorn claims our attention to this extent, because in the four collections of songs that best illustrate the transition of the lied to the immediate post-baroque phase, his poetry is of increasing and finally dominating importance. These collections all appeared some ten years before the death of Bach and before Goethe's birth, around 1740. Hagedorn's *Oden und Lieder* makes this a point of critical change in German poetry. In music it was hardly less decisive, if only for the reason that, roughly speaking, it marks the stage at which the use of the figured bass begins, with far-reaching implications, to enter its period of decline.

In 1736, under the pseudonym Sperontes, Johann Sigismund Scholze published a collection of songs entitled *Singende Muse an der Pleiße*, which reached a fifth edition by 1751. Except for a number of poems by Günther, the texts are by Scholze himself. He used existing melodies, presumptuously described in the advertisement of the work at the Leipzig Fair of 1736 as 'the best and most well-known'. An occasional tendency in so good a composer as Erlebach to fit words to a tune to which they do not easily go, could suggest that a rather more casual view of the relationship of poetry and song had begun to creep into the strophic continuo lied. The *Musikalische Rüstkammer* is more obviously symptomatic, but it is the *Singende Muse an der Pleiße* that most clearly illustrates the position in the final phase of the dying baroque. In some pieces the relationship may be open to only minor criticism, but in many the obviously instrumental derivation Ex. 33 of the tune makes the result ungainly and disturbing.

To this feature of the *Singende Muse an der Pleiße* exception was taken by Johann Friedrich Gräfe, who had close contacts with the Gottsched circle, and who in 1737, a year after the first instalment of Sperontes's work, published his *Sammlung verschiedener auserlesener Oden*. A second edition appeared in 1740 and a third in 1743; the second part was published in 1740, the third in 1741, and the fourth two years later. Gräfe makes a dig at Sperontes's practice of fitting his texts to existing tunes when in the foreword he stresses that in the case of his own songs 'melodies have been provided by the most famous masters'. He boasts that 'the music for the songs is quite new and composed specially for the texts', and, stressing his respect for the words, that the collection is by someone 'who loves both music and poetry'. When he attacks what he regards as the ornate pretentiousness of Sperontes's frontispiece, one could gloss his view with a reference to Gottsched's idea that what is rational is what is natural, and what is natural is also rational—an outlook which, despising superfluous decoration, aims at a middle-class kind of simplicity. The two editions of the first part were dedicated to Mariane von Ziegler, a member of Gottsched's circle and Leipzig's leading poetess, and the second part to the most formidable blue-stocking of the Enlightenment, Frau Gottsched. She is represented by one poem, Mariane von Ziegler by nine, and Gottsched himself by fifteen.

Though Gräfe speaks of his composers as the 'most famous masters', only C. P. E. Bach would now qualify for the description. Still under thirty, he had been called to the court of Frederick the Great as harpsichordist and had composed a considerable quantity of instrumental music. But his setting of a text by Mariane von Ziegler (first published in her *Vermischte Schriften*, 1739, and later used by Haydn in his *Zwölf Lieder*, Vienna, 1782) is classified as his first song.[1] It is entitled *Schäferlied*, and was later included in his *Oden mit Melodien* (Berlin, 1762). Whereas in Handel's *Süße Stille, sanfte Quelle* dissonance conveys man's yearning for nature's peace, in this *Schäferlied*, reprinted in Friedländer's book on eighteenth-century German songs, man is at one with nature by the act of assuming the roles of shepherd and shepherdess. Dissonance, as at *aus den Gründen* and *Sagt, was er mir mitgenommen*, does not challenge this pretence. It merely dramatizes feeling in the context of a playful masquerade. The melody is flowing and simple, and so, by post-baroque standards, natural.

Gräfe uses an occasional poem by baroque writers, but the tone is set by the post-baroque texts, including two by Hagedorn. Telemann had used a poem of Hagedorn in his *Singe-, Spiel- und Generalbaß-übungen* in 1734, and there are five in Telemann's more important *Vier und zwanzig, theils ernsthafte, theils scherzende, Oden*, published in Hamburg in 1741. Most of the texts, mainly by Ebert, Stoppe, and Dreyer, exemplify less the anacreontic trends of the time than the belief that by escaping to nature one could live simply and rationally. The *24 Oden* was published the year before the first set of Hagedorn's *Oden und Lieder*, so that Hagedorn too is referred to in Telemann's remark in the preface that the collection contains 'as far as I know, material not previously printed'.

Ebert is a particularly dreary versifier, whose visions of the pastoral life always raise a smile:

> An dieser schattenreichen Linde,
> Wo schon mein Vater schlief und sung,
> In deren grünlich braune Rinde
> Ich neulich Phyllis Namen schlung,
> In diesem Klee, an diesem Bache,
> Der meine Schafe tränkt und kühlt,
> Hier lieg ich, spiele, singe, lache
> Und schlafe, wenn ich gnug gespielt.

---

[1] G. Busch, *C. P. E. Bach und seine Lieder*, Regensburg, 1957, i. 40.

Ich sehe meine Schafe weiden
Und weide mit, da ich dies seh.
Ich weide mich in tausend Freuden
Und sie sich in dem fettsten Klee.
Oft laß ich Stimm und Leier klingen,
Dann essen sie noch eins so sehr,
Und hör ich wieder auf zu singen,
So blöken sie, und fordern mehr.

The last stanza of this poem contrasts the shepherd's existence with more sophisticated ways of life:

Laß andre nur nach Reichtum streben,
Das Glücke gibt und nimmt ihn nur.
Mir ist ein Baum und Bach gegeben,
Und diese gab mir die Natur.
Laß andre weit und prächtig wohnen,
Ich habe doch noch größern Raum.
Sie liegen auf erhabenen Thronen;
Ich unter einem hohen Baum.

Dreyer tells us that those who devote themselves to love and nature have all the advantages:

Wer der Vorurteile Macht
Und der Laster Reiz verlacht,
Wer sich von dem Pöbel trennet,
Wer Natur und Wollust kennet,
Und sich dann der Liebe weiht;
Lebt in einer güldnen Zeit

—and Stoppe too is out for the delights of the simple life:

Statt mein Glück empor zu treiben,
Mag mein Wohlsein in der Welt
Auf der Mittelstraße bleiben,
Weil man da nicht leichte fällt.
Wenn ich meine Notdurft habe,
Nach dem andern frag ich nicht.
Wohl mir, wenn mir bis zum Grabe
Stets der Überfluß gebricht!

Just as Dreyer's poem speaks of the need both to despise vice and prejudice and also to stand apart from the mob, the title of Stoppe's poem would be translated as 'the middle way between wealth and poverty', but *Mittelstand* also denotes middle class. The ambiguity is unintentional, but very appropriate, for the texts of the *24 Oden*, defying the extremes of aristocratic pretension and plebeian vulgarity, proclaim complacently middle-class values, contentment, moderation, honesty, and sincerity:

> Setzt mich niemand bei die Sterne,
>   Leb ich doch auch ohne Spott,
> Kennt mich niemand in der Ferne,
>   Kennt mich doch der liebe Gott.
> Laßt den Ehrentempel schließen!
> Ich verlange ja nicht hin.
> Gnug! daß meine Nachbarn wissen,
>   Daß ich treu und ehrlich bin.

Nature is the uncorrupting environment best suited for the cultivation of the sought-after virtues:

> Himmel, Sterne, Feld und Bäume,
> Sind auch meinetwegen da,
> Und die Dummheit eurer Träume,
> Blöde Seelen, kenn ich ja.
> Martert und beklaget euch,
> Glaubt, das größte Königreich
> Ist nicht meiner Ruhe gleich.

Rivers and streams offer something better than beer, what nature provides is good for you, and you get it free:

> In den Bächen, in den Flüssen
>   Braut uns die Natur das Bier,
> Das wir ohn Entgelt genießen;
>   Denn wir zahlen nichts dafür.
> Wasser! du gesunder Trank!
> Du erquickst die matten Säfte;
> Durch des Bieres wilde Kräfte
>   Wird oft mancher sterbenskrank.

This poem on the theme of 'the contented pastoral life' recommends nature as the best escape from sophistication and corruption, and also from the pretentious artifice of castrati singers:

> Hier entbehr ich der Kastraten,
>   Weil ihr Lied zu kostbar klingt.
> Meiner Lust ist leicht geraten,
>   Wenn das Chor der Vögel singt;
>   Wenn der nahgelegne Wald,
> Nebst dem niedrigen Gesträuche,
> Um die ufervollen Teiche
>   Wie ein Orgelwerk erschallt

—and from money as the root of all evil:

> Wird mir bei dem Schäferstande
>     Gleich kein Kapital bewußt;
> Gnug! ein Armer auf dem Lande
>     Braucht kein Geld zu seiner Lust.
> Mein mit Gott zufriedner Sinn
> Darf nach keinen Schätzen streben,
> Weil ich bei dem armen Leben
>     Reicher als ein König bin

—and the hypocrisy of urban life:

> Laßt die Städter sich erheben,
>     Wenn ihr Kleid von Silber strotzt.
> Wenn ihr scheinbar goldnes Leben
>     Auf das Geld im Beutel trotzt:
>     Trotzdem wir auf unser Feld,
> Das, sobald die Sonne blitzet,
> Früh soviel Juwelen schwitzet,
>     Deren Zahl kein Mensch behält.

The anacreontic poetry in the *24 Oden* has an obvious relationship to these aspects. Wine, like nature, bestows peace, Ebert observes— though elsewhere, as we have seen, water is preferred to alcohol:

> Fürst und König der Getränke,
> Du der Erde best Geschenke,
>     Stifter vieler Ruh!
> Wer macht, daß wir viele Plagen
> Standhaft und gelassen tragen?
>     Hoffen nur, und du

—it destroys care:

> Gram und Sorg und Grillen fliehen,
> Scherz und Freud und Hoffnung ziehen
>     Wieder in die Brust.
> Man sieht Gläser Gläsern winken.
> Man glaubt nur den Wein zu trinken,
>     Und trinkt lauter Lust

—and it unites people:

> Lasset Feind und Feinde kriegen,
> Und verlieren, und auch siegen;
>     Uns besiegt der Wein.
> Oder laßt das Blutvergießen;
> Dieses Blut wird edler Fließen.
>     Setztet euch, schenkt ein!

Hagedorn expresses the last idea in the following poem, *Die Ursache der Kriege*:

> Mein! sage mir, warum die Fürsten fechten?
> Fragt Görgel den Gevatter Hein.
> Der lacht und spricht: Wenn sie, wie wir, gedächten,
> Sie stellten alle Händel ein.
> Wenn sie, wie wir, nur oft zusammen zechten,
> Sie würden Freund und Brüder sein.

The *24 Oden* is dedicated to Scheibe, the musical theorist most directly concerned with the Enlightenment, and it was probably respect for Scheibe's taste that led Telemann in the foreword ruefully to profess that 'I have by no means achieved a straightforward simplicity (*Bathos*) or succeeded in composing in an ordinary, everyday manner', that he had not mastered *die Kunst, niedrig zu schreiben*. Like Gottsched, he pokes fun at opera, praises Saint-Evremont for his attacks upon it, and calls it a 'fatuous distraction'. It would be well, he says, if the 'artificial *ha-ha-ha, he-he-he* of singers had been banished from the stage and its place taken by the simplicity of *Nun ruhen alle Wälder*'. Probably it is a sneer at Sperontes when he remarks that his tunes 'don't demand the high register of a wren or the low notes of a bittern, but stick to the middle way', and the sub-title describes them as 'easy melodies convenient for all voices'. Johann Ernst Bach, in the preface to Adlung's *Anleitung zur musikalischen Gelahrtheit* (Erfurt, 1758), calls Telemann's church music 'simple' (*leicht*) and '*natural*', and this could be applied to the *24 Oden*. But Telemann is a very transitional figure. His chamber music combines music typical of the post-baroque 'galant' style, particularly in the slow movements, with a manner more representative of *le style continu*.

Usually, as one would expect, these songs move by easy intervals and present hardly any problems to the performer. When they sometimes suggest instrumental associations, these are not such as to make them awkward for the voice so much as to reduce their interest for the singer, and only occasionally is there a slight reminder of the weak- Ex. 34 nesses characteristic of Sperontes.

A year later a collection of twenty-five songs appeared called *Sammlung Neuer Oden und Lieder*. A second part with thirty songs was published in 1744. The work was completed by a further fifteen songs in 1752, and this revealed Görner as the composer and Hagedorn as author of the texts. His poems in the first two parts appeared there for the first time, and he also wrote the preface to the first part, a treatise on folk-song, later reprinted in Marpurg's *Historisch-kritische Beiträge zur Aufnahme der Musik*. He was also associated with the preparation of the second part, but then for some reason withdrew his collaboration. But Görner included in the third part poems that Hagedorn had meanwhile published in the 1747 edition of his poems. As to Görner, he was born in 1702 near Chemnitz, and died in Hamburg in 1762. He studied at Leipzig University, visited various courts, and then settled in Hamburg, where he became master of music at the cathedral and collaborated with Telemann in his musical serial *Der getreue Musicmeister*.

Like Telemann, Görner labels each song with a term descriptive of its mood. (This habit is indirectly related to Scheibe's principle, which Lessing commends in the *Hamburgische Dramaturgie*[1] and Quantz affirms,[2] that incidental music for a drama must accord with its general character.) In both the *24 Oden* and the *Sammlung Neuer Oden und Lieder* the emphasis is on gay and gentle feelings. Epithets like *munter, freudig, lustig* are typical, and both men favour *unschuldig, gelassen, süß, angenehm, reizend, lieblich, schmeichelnd*, and *zärtlich*. Reference to the more delicate and tender feelings become proportionately more frequent in Görner's second part, and again in the third. For tenderness, love, and joy, we are now told in one of Telemann's songs, are among the cardinal virtues:

> Wen Einfalt und Wahn nicht betrügen,
> Der glaubet und weiß und empfindt:
> Daß Zärtlichkeit, Lieb und Vergnügen
> Wahrhaftige Tugenden sind.

The larger and more dramatic issues are pushed aside, and attention is focused on simple and easily accessible forms of experience, on emotions requiring for their fulfilment nothing that a limited and familiar environment cannot provide. The tunes are, if anything, more obviously vocal than Telemann's, but even so not all of them are without a suggestion of instrumental associations.

One of them is a setting of Hagedorn's poem *Der Morgen*:

> Uns lockt die Morgenröte
> In Busch und Wald,
> Wo schon der Hirten Flöte
> Ins Land erschallt.
> Die Lerche steigt und schwirret,
> Von Lust erregt;
> Die Taube lacht und girret,
> Die Wachtel schlägt.

[1] 67. Stück.  [2] Ed. cit., p. 224.

Die Hügel und die Weide
  Stehn aufgehellt,
Und Fruchtbarkeit und Freude
  Beblümt das Feld.
Der Schmelz der grünen Flächen
  Glänzt voller Pracht,
Und von den klaren Bächen
  Entweicht die Nacht.

Der Hügel weiße Bürde,
  Der Schafe Zucht,
Drängt sich aus Stall und Hürde
  Mit froher Flucht.
Seht, wie der Mann der Herde
  Den Morgen fühlt,
Und auf der frischen Erde
  Den Buhler spielt!

Der Jäger macht schon rege
  Und hetzt das Reh
Durch blutbetriefte Wege,
  Durch Busch und Klee.
Sein Hifthorn gibt das Zeichen;
  Man eilt herbei:
Gleich schallt aus allen Sträuchen
  Das Jagdgeschrei.

Doch Phyllis Herz erbebet
  Bei dieser Lust;
Nur Zärtlichkeit belebet
  Die sanfte Brust.
Laß uns die Täler suchen,
  Geliebtes Kind,
Wo wir von Berg und Buchen
  Umschlossen sind!

Erkenne dich im Bilde
  Von jener Flur!
Sei stets, wie dies Gefilde,
  Schön durch Natur;
Erwünschter als der Morgen,
  Hold wie sein Strahl;
So frei von Stolz und Sorgen
  Wie dieses Tal!

This has the same metrical pattern as Opitz's *Ach Liebste laß uns eilen*—and also, incidentally, as one of Goethe's rococo poems, *Erwache Friederike*, which, reflecting its popularity, was probably written to Görner's melody. In the poem quoted at the beginning of this chapter Hagedorn praises Opitz's poetry for being close to nature, a comment which is justified only as a way of contrasting Opitz with Hofmannswaldau, whom Hagedorn is attacking. In fact, Hagedorn's *Der Morgen* serves to show how small a part by comparison Opitz finds for nature in his poem. Hagedorn renounces metaphor for descriptive statements, and the theme of eternity has vanished. Whereas Opitz speaks of the impermanence of natural things, Hagedorn sees nature as our model, imitation of it as man's noblest task. Beauty is identified not with the transcendental world, as in Hofmannswaldau's poem:

> So wirst du leicht in diesen Port gelangen,
> Da Ewigkeit und Schönheit dich umfaßt,

but with nature itself:

> Sei stets, wie dies Gefilde,
> Schön durch Natur.

Opitz enjoys the pleasures of life amid worried preoccupation with transience and death, but for Hagedorn, uninhibited by metaphysical cares, to be in nature is to be free, and Görner's setting is as relaxed and idyllic as the poem.       Ex.

Just as Hagedorn reduces nature to its cosier aspects, protective and enfolding:

> Laß uns die Täler suchen,
> Geliebtes Kind,
> Wo wir von Berg und Buchen
> Umschlossen sind,

the setting, similarly unconcerned with transience and mortality, falls comfortably and reassuringly into a series of short and homely units. There is a link here with the Berlin School, illustrated by Johann Peter Schulz when, in the preface to the second edition in 1784 of his *Lieder im Volkston*, he said that his aim was to compose 'in a popular rather than a sophisticated way and with the greatest natural simplicity in order to give people the cosily reassuring feeling that they were on familiar ground'—to give them *den Schein des Bekannten*. Called upon to do no more than reflect the mood of carefree and graceful contentment, Görner's music can be satisfied with an easily flowing melody on a foundation so simple as to aspire to no serious expressive function— an aspect noted by Marpurg in Telemann's *24 Oden*, when with a little exaggeration he said that they 'achieve their effect without the bass'.[1] This feature alone, though the bass is still figured, indicates that we have here crossed the frontier to a different age.

[1] Quoted by M. Friedländer, *Das deutsche Lied im 18. Jahrhundert*, i. 82.

# EPILOGUE

## The Heart's Assurance

ON this side of the border the changed attitude to nature inevitably involved a conception of language, and of its relation to music, other than that which had prevailed in the baroque. Nature, no longer opening out into metaphysical vistas, is cherished for its own intrinsic realities, which, like the birds, the sheep, and the shepherd in Hagedorn's poem, become worthy and even exciting in their own right. The language, in which this experience of nature is expressed, points to nothing beyond the immediate experience. Since it could be argued that music could not as directly as language express the experience of things cherished and enjoyed, anxiety was expressed that music, at home in the sphere of feeling rather than objects, better at suggestion than definition, might interfere with what poetry wanted to say. Gottsched declared that 'only a poet's words can explain what the composer wishes to convey',[1] and Mattheson, in the *Kern melodischer Wissenschaft*,[2] advised the composer against 'approaching too close to the meaning of the words, even if it costs him the finest fugue ever written'.

The conception of song as an easy tune over a simple bass was coming to be widely championed in Germany, as by Christian Gottfried Krause, whose treatise *Von der musicalischen Poesie* appeared in 1752. Krause, a central figure of the Berlin School, a lawyer by profession and in his spare time composer and theorist, was a typical minor representative of the Enlightenment, a great believer in education and the brotherhood of man. Reflecting these ideas, music for him was primarily a sociable activity, uniting men beyond the distinctions of class, creed, or calling, and song was above all melody, and melody of a kind suitable for informal and convivial company. Germans, he noted, were everywhere interested in music, but too often one heard only operatic arias—not the kind of music, he thought, apt for lighthearted song 'that anyone could sing without difficulty and that could be sung without a keyboard or any sort of accompaniment'. If Germans 'composed their songs using only their voices and without

---

[1] Quoted by W. Steinecke, *Die Parodie in der Musik*, Wolfenbüttel and Berlin, 1934, p. 141.                                         [2] p. 108.

using the keyboard, and also without thinking of putting a bass to them, then the taste for singing will become widespread in our country, and will everywhere introduce a mood of joy and happiness'.[1] Scheibe lent his greater authority to a similar view when he said in 1739 that 'the tune of a song must flow easily, purely, and above all naturally, in order that it can immediately be reproduced without difficulty by anyone without musical experience'.[2]

Views such as these, restricting the role of music in song to the simple task of providing an easy and tuneful melody, have various implications, reflecting amongst other things the advent of social ideals more democratic than those paramount in the baroque. In a sense too they follow logically from the development of poetry itself in the baroque age. The growth of German poetry in the period that saw the baroque lied burgeon, flower, and fade records the process by which it came to emancipate itself from music. This consisted in the creation of poetry that required only to be spoken or read, and, artificial though the means may often have been, of a kind of poetry in which the actual music, on which in the sixteenth century it had in the main relied, was replaced by 'an intensified and purely verbal music'. This demanded the 'strictly controlled rhythmic discipline which is alien to folk-song because, since it was sung, it did not need it'[3]—and it required too those forbiddingly pedantic rules about strophic forms, elisions, iambs, trochees, and the rest, which out of this context seem only a bookman's distraction. It was no coincidence that it was when the baroque had accomplished its task in this respect that the demand came to be put forward that in song the music should be simple enough to let the words tell their own story in their own way.

The beginning of the decline, from about 1740, of the figured bass as a paramount principle of musical organization was only one feature of a changing situation. This was the time too when the baroque forms of fugue, partita, and suite begin to become archaic, 'when the rigid tone of the organ and harpsichord begins to give way to the more sensitive and personal notes of the hammerklavier', when 'in the Mannheim style form comes to be seen as development, and instrumentation becomes subtler'—so that in a comparison of Rameau's overture to *Castor et Pollux* (1737) with the *Sinfonies d'Allemagne*

---

[1] Quoted by Kretzschmar, op. cit., p. 235.

[2] Quoted by E. D. Lindner, *Geschichte des deutschen Liedes im 18. Jahrhundert*, Leipzig, 1871, p. 30.

[3] H. A. Korff, *Geist der Goethezeit*, i, Leipzig, 1923, p. 175.

that were causing such a sensation in Paris, the older style of Rameau could be described as *d'une teneur*, because 'les nuances du doux au fort, continuellement et graduellement menagées, sont encore des finesses de l'art, dont Rameau faisait peu d'usage'.[1] In song the change of direction here indicated is first significantly marked by C. P. E. Bach's *Geistliche Arien und Lieder* (1752), settings of Gellert's poetry, in which the music is meticulously moulded to the changing nuances of single words and phrases. When this collection appeared, C. P. E. Bach had only recently published his *Versuch über die wahre Art, das Clavier zu spielen*, embodying the principle that music is an expression of private and personal experience—'one must play from the soul (*aus der Seele muß man spielen*)'.[2] As one critic has nicely put it, the difference, as compared with the baroque, is between 'expressing something' and 'expressing oneself', between *sich ausdrücken* and *etwas ausdrücken*.[3] But he is wrong in attributing to C. P. E. Bach's views direct links with *Sturm und Drang*; their association is rather with the 'age of sensibility', in which feeling, even to the extent of tearful sentimentality, came to be cherished and enjoyed for its own sake.

Baroque music is, it is true, often passionate by any standard, but always, as in baroque architecture, the feeling is controlled by more objective principles of order than the post-baroque world could easily accept, and this applies to poetry as well. Whereas during the seventeenth century verse had been shaped to rather mechanical rhythms and to effects gained from the play of words, the flux of feeling itself could now begin to be thought of as musical. Thus, in the time of Mozart, in the youth of Goethe, Klopstock could say that the perfection of lyrical poetry resided 'in the melodious course of passion or feeling'.[4] As to song, it was to be 'man's discourse with his own heart, with God, and with the whole of nature', and, no longer merely 'a calculated arrangement of notes and chords', its essence was to be 'euphony', dancing to 'the melody of the heart'.[5]

[1] W. Gurlitt, 'Form in der Musik als Zeitgestaltung', *Akademie der Wissenschaften und der Literatur in Mainz, Abhandlungen der Geistes- und Sozialwissenschaftlichen Klasse*, 1954.
[2] 3. Hauptstück, section 7.
[3] H. H. Eggebrecht, 'Das Ausdrucksprinzip im musikalischen Sturm und Drang', *Deutsche Vierteljahrschrift für Literaturwissenschaft und Geistesgeschichte*, xxix, 1955, p. 330.
[4] In his essay on 'Volkslieder', Bibliographisches Institut edition of his *Werke*, ii. 315.
[5] In 'Von deutscher Art und Kunst', ibid., p. 64. The contrast is between *aufgezähltes Harmonienkunststück* and *Wohlklang*.

# APPENDIX A

*Musical Examples*

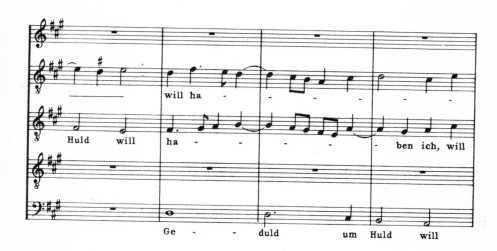

From: Ludwig Senfl, *Sämtliche Werke,* ii, Möseler Verlag, Wolfenbüttel and Zürich.

# 2

Mein Mund der singt,_____ mein Herz vor

Mein Mund der singt,_____ (etc.)

Mein Mund der singt, (etc.)

Trau-rern weint, mein Herz_____ vor Trau-rern weint, So

bös-lich sind, so bös-lich sind mein Mund und Herz ver-eint.

Daß solchs konnt sein, hätt ich nie-mals ge-

-meint, hätt ich nie-mals ge-meint -meint.

Wenn ich\_\_\_\_\_ ge - denk der Stund, da ich muß schei -

Wenn ich\_\_\_\_\_ ge - denk *(etc.)*

Wenn ich\_\_\_\_\_ ge - denk *(etc.)*

-den, da ich muß schei - den, Wie dann ge - scheh - en

wird in kur - zen Ta - gen, Mein Herz im Leib will mir vor

Leid, will mir vor Leid, will mir vor Leid, will

mir vor Leid - - - - ver - za - gen. -gen.

# 4

FIRST CHOIR

Mein Lieb will mit mir krie - gen, Hat sich ge - rüst zur Schlacht.

Mein Lieb will mit mir krie - gen, (etc.)

Mein Lieb will mit mir krie - gen, (etc.)

Mein Lieb will mit mir krie - gen, (etc.)

SECOND CHOIR

Mein Lieb will mit mir

Mein Lieb will mit mir

Mein Lieb will mit mir

Mein Lieb will mit mir

Läßt ih - re Fah - nen flie - gen, Trotz

krie - gen, Hat sich ge - rüst zur Schlacht.

krie - gen, (etc.)

krie - gen, (etc.)

krie - gen, (etc.)

viel

bin durch-schos - sen Mit ih - ren Äu - glein zart,

Blut hab ich ver - gos - sen, Töd - lich - ver - wun - det

From: *Denkmäler deutscher Tonkunst, Zweite Folge: Denkmäler der Tonkunst in Bayern,* v, ii, Breitkopf and Härtel.

# 5

# 7

From: *Denkmäler deutscher Tonkunst,* Zweite Folge: *Denkmäler der Tonkunst in Bayern,* v, ii, Breitkopf and Härtel.

# 8

Mir - til - lo mein, dein De - li - a, Die dich von

Mir - til - lo mein, (etc.)

Mir - til - lo mein, (etc.)

Her - zen lie - bet, In dei-ne Treu und

Gra - ti - a Sich dir heut ganz er - gie -

-bet. Mir - -bet. Die Göttr und

Nym - phen all zu - gleich Mit dir sich hoch er - freu — en, Im Wald untr ein - nem grün Ge - sträuch Führn ein - nen lu - - - - stgen Rei - hen, Die -hen.

# 9

O Ster-nen Äu - ge - lein! O Sei-den Hä - re-

O Ster - nen Äu - ge - lein! O Sei - den Hä - re-

O Ster - nen Äu - ge - lein! *(etc.)*

-lein! O Ro - sen Wän - ge - lein! Ko - ral - len Lip - pe-

-lein! *(etc.)*

-lein! O Per - len Zäh - ne - lein! O

Ho - nig - zün - ge - lein! -lein! O Per - le - mut - ter Öh - re-

## 10

All Leut und Tier - - so ihr hier - um
Wol - let ver - blei - - ben still und stumm,

hal - tet in der Re - vier, Förd - rist bit ich_____
fleis - sig zu hö - ren mir,

schön Herr-schrin mein, wollt hier-zu un - - ver-dross-en sein.

From: W. Vetter, *Das frühdeutsche Lied*, Helios Verlag.

## 11

Ach Lieb - ste laß uns___ ei - len, Wir ha - ben

Zeit: Es scha-det das Ver - wei - len Uns bei - der -

-seit. Der___ ed - len___ Schön - heit Ga - ben Fliehn Fuß für

Fuß, Daß al-les was wir ha - ben Ver-schwin-den muß. muß.

From: W. Vetter, *Das frühdeutsche Lied*, Helios Verlag.

# 12

Phyl - lis, die mich vor - mals lie - bet, Der ich auch mein Herz be - dacht,

Hat mich jet - zund so be - trü - bet, Daß ich kei - ner Freu - den acht;

Soll ich sie nicht wie - der - sehn, So ist es um — mich ge - schehn.

From: *Denkmäler deutscher Tonkunst,* Erste Folge, xii, Breitkopf and Härtel.

# 13

Mein lieb - stes Seel - chen laßt uns le - ben So lang wir. noch im

Le - ben sein! Bald bricht der schlim - me Tod her - ein,

So müs - sen wir das u - ber - ge - ben Was und so sanft und

lin - de tat, Was uns so oft er - göt - zet hat.

From: *Denkmäler deutscher Tonkunst,* Erste Folge, xii, Breitkopf and Härtel.

# 14

O — der rau-hen Grau - sam-keit!

O der rau-hen Grau - sam-keit!

O der rau-hen Grau - sam-keit!

Die nur Seuf - zen je - der - zeit Mit viel

Seuf - zen häuft, Mit viel Seuf - zen

häuft. O des Le - bens oh - ne Le - ben, Das zum

To - de läuft, Das in Zit - tern

From: *Denkmäler deutscher Tonkunst,* Erste Folge, xii, Breitkopf and Härtel.

# 15

Seht doch wie der Rhein-wein tanzt, in dem schö-nen Gla - se,
Wie er hin und wie-der ranzt, und kriecht in die Na - se,

daß man vom Ge-ru-che bald, dumm und dämsch muß wer - den,

nein, was hat er für Ge-walt ü - ber uns auf Er - den.

RITORNELLO

*(etc.)*

# 16

Ihr schö - nen Au - gen! ihr hel - ler Glanz! Wer

wird euch tau - gen, ihr blen - det ganz! Ihr kla - ren Ster - ne scheint

ge - gen mir, Als wie von fer - nen des Him - mels Zier.

RITORNELLO

From: *Denkmäler deutscher Tonkunst,* Erste Folge, xix, Breitkopf and Härtel.

## 17

Wo muß der schö-ne Jä - ger sein, A - do - nis mei-ne_ See - le?
Er eilt dem blo-ßen Wil - de nach, Und ich des-sel-ben Schat - ten.
Ich ha-be sei-nen Hut ge-sehn Und mehr von ihm im_ Wal - de.

Um den ich in ver - lieb-ter Pein Mich of-te plag und quä - le.
Sein Herz und Sin-nen sein die Schmach,So mich sonst bei sich hat - ten.
O Him-mel, laß es doch ge-schehn,Daß ich ihn fin-de bal - de.

RITORNELLO I
*Adagio*

O— bit - tre Pein! Ü - ber die wohl nichts kann sein. Ein— wil - des
O— su - ßes Herz! Sonst ein Scherz und nun mein Schmerz, Muß dich ein
O— her - be Qual! Die mir als ein Don - ner - strahl. Das— Mark in

From: *Denkmäler deutscher Tonkunst*, Erste Folge, xix, Breitkopf and Härtel.

# 18

Fleug, fleug, fleug Psy-che, fleug, fleug, fleug, fleug, Cu - pi - do will nicht

mehr dein ei - gen sein. Fleug, fleug Psy-che, fleug, fleug, fleug, Cu - pi - do

will nicht mehr dein ei - gen sein. Hier hat er sich in die-sen hel - len Au -

-gen der zar - ten Braut ein Wohn - haus auf - ge-baut, Der zar - ten Braut ein

Wohn - haus auf - ge - baut. Dir, dir, dir, dir, dir,

dir, dir, dir, dir, o schön - ste Zier, Er - wirbt er nur al -

-lein der-gleich-en Ehr Und schätzt dich gleich der wun - der-vol-

-len Psy - che, Von der er neu - lich wic - he.

*Adagio*
Wo nun Cu - pi - do sit - zet, Und in der Stir - ne

*Presto*
blit - zet, Da muß die sü - ße Lie - bes-pein Voll Hitz und Feu -

- - - - - - - - er sein.

RITORNELLO I

Frei-lich, frei-lich ist die Glut, So da-hier in eu-rem Mut

Und in al-len A-dern bren-net,___ Von der Ve-nus

an - ge-zünd't, Weil sie, gar zu lie - bes Kind, Gleich nach eu-ren Au-gen ren - net.

RITORNELLO II

Hier laßt ihr die Lie - bes - flamm  Eu - rem lie - bsten Bräu - ti - gam,

Gleich nach sei - nem Her - zen schie - ßen. Er hin - ge - gen

6  5  6  ♯  6  4  ♯  ♯  ♯  6  ♯  6

lacht und denkt, Was ihn itz-und hei-mlich kränkt, Bald vollkommen zu ge-nie-ßen.

7  6  ♯  ♯6  6  ♯  6  4  ♯

**RITORNELLO II**

6  ♯  67 6 ♯  6  6  6
♯  ♯

♯  4  ♯ ♯  5  6  ♯  ♯  4  ♯
♭  3

So ge-nie-ße frisch und frei Dei-ne Lust, du schö-nes zwei,

Und er-lan-ge dein Ver-lan - gen, Was der Him-mel

Gu-tes gibt, Sei in dich zu-gleich ver-liebt, So kannst du ver-gnu-get pran-gen.

RITORNELLO

Wir wün-schen euch und eu - - - rem Her - zen Ein recht er-
-freu - - - lich Lie-bes-scher-zen, Ein Glü - cke
von des Him-mels Hö - he, Daß al - les Trau-ern von euch ge - he, Ein
süß und an-gen-eh-mes Lie - ben, Das al - le Welt so oft ge-
-trie - ben, Ein Herz und Sinn und ei - ne____ See - le, So lan - ge
wir in die - ser____ Höh - le Die hoch - ge - schätz - ten
Him - mels-ga - ben, Mit Freu-den kön-nen bei uns ha - ben. *ut supra*
Fleug, Psyche

From: *Denkmäler deutscher Tonkunst*, Erste Folge, xix, Breitkopf and Härtel.

## 19

Do - rin - de, du präch - tigst auf Er - den Von

Tu - gend, Zucht, Schön-heit, Ge - bar - den, Laß mich dei-nen Die - ner sein.

Ich lauf ihr nach Mit Weh und Ach, Schau an mein Herz, Das vol-ler

Schmerz In Flammen steht! Kein Tag ver-geht, Ich seuf-ze nach dir mein Täu-be-lein.

## 20

O E - wig - keit, du Don-ner - wort, O Schwert, das durch die
O E - wig - keit, Zeit oh - ne Zeit, Ich weiß vor gro - ßer

See - le bohrt, O An - fang son - der En - de. Mein
Trau - rig - keit Nicht wo ich hin mich wen - de.

ganz er-schroc-knes Herz er-bebt, Daß mir die Zung am Gau-men klebt.

## 21

Laß Seuf-zen, laß Kla-gen, wer la-chen nicht kann, Laß jam-mer-lich
Mein Hoff-nung, die drin-get mit Freu-den he - ran, Sie lä-sset mich

heu-len die tö-richten Sin - nen.
end-lich mit Eh-ren ge-win - nen.

Mich, der ich ge-krie-get in

Jam-mer und Not, Hab end-lich ge-sie-get, mein Trau-ren ist tot.

## 22

Lus-tig zu Fel-de mit Pfer-den und Wa - gen, Hoh-let die

Frü-chte, so Tel-lus ge - tra - gen. Spa-ret das Fei - ren,

fül-let die Scheu-ern, Wei-zen und Rog-gen und Ger-sten bringt

ein! Flo-ri-dan sel-ber will Ern-te-mann sein.

## 23

Glim-mert ihr Ste - rne, Schim-mert von fe - rne, Blink-ert nicht trü - be,

Flink-ert, zu - lie - be Die-ser er - freu-li - chen lie - bli - chen Zeit.

La-chet, ihr Him - mel, Ma-chet Ge - tüm - mel, Re - gnet uns Se - gen,

Se-gnet den Re - gen, Der uns in Freu-de ver - wan-delt das Leid.

## 24

Ach kein als dei - ne Lieb er - töt - et mei - ne Pein. Die Pein ist

gleich - falls mein. Ver-stü-ben doch die Berg', und (etc.)

## 25

Ihr Bü - cher, mei - ne Freu-de, du lei-chte Fe - der du,

die ich zum Schrei - ben schnei-de, hört mei-nem Seu - fzen zu.

# 26

## I. *Domine, usque quo?*

1 Ach, wie lang, O Gott, mein Gott, wie lan - ge, Willst du dich von mein - en

Trän - en keh - ren Und kein - er Bit - te mich ge - währ - en?

Ach, wie ist mir doch so— hef - tig ban - ge, Daß du mich nun ganz aus

dein - em Her - zen schleußt und in grund - lo - se Schmer - zen,

Oh - ne Trost ver - sink - en läßt! Soll ich, Herr, dein Ant - litz nicht mehr

schau - en? Hab ich nicht, O Hei - land, mein Ver - trau - en

Stets auf dich ge - grün - det fest?

2  Ach, wie lange soll in tausend Plagen
Unter deines Grimmes Donnerkeilen
Und höllenheißen Schwefelpfeilen
Ich mein immerwährend Weh beklagen?
Ach, wie müd ist mein Gemüt von Sorgen,
Welches plötzlich alle Morgen
Angst und Elend überfällt.
Ist wohl eine Trübsal zu ergründen,
Wird man auch ein Unglück können finden,
Das mich nicht in Klauen hält?


3  Doch ich möchte dies noch alles leiden,
Daß sich aber meine Feind erheben,
Weil ich in höchster Qual muß leben,
Daß so fröhlich jauchzen, die mich neiden,
Dies, dies will mir Leib und Geist durchdringen
Und mich zum Verzweifeln bringen.
Mein Gott, ach, mein großer Gott,
Wofern dein Gemüte zu erweichen,
Wofern eine Gnade zu erreichen,
Schaue doch auf meinen Spott!


4  Welt, ade! Es ist um mich geschehen,
Meine Kraft weicht, und die Augen brechen,
Die Zunge kann kein Wort mehr sprechen,
Der Tod hat mich ihm zum Raub ersehen.
Ach, Herr, einen Strahl nur deiner Güte
Wünscht mein sterbendes Gemüte.
Brich doch an, du Lebenslicht!
Mein Feind wird es seiner Macht zuschreiben,
Wo ich muß im Staube liegen bleiben,
Dulde doch sein Pochen nicht.

5    Nun, ich weiß, du wirst mir nicht abschlagen,
Was ich jetzt mit halberstarrter Zungen
Und pfnüchzend habe vorgedrungen;
Deine Gnade kennet kein Versagen.
Alle Welt weiß deine Treu zu preisen,
Die du pflegest zu erweisen,
Wenn kein Mittel mehr zu sehn.
Herr, ich glaub, ich will nach so viel Schreien
Über deine Wohltat mich erfreuen,
Ja ich weiß, es wird geschehn.

I Was ist die Welt, Die mich bis - her mit ihr er Pracht be - tö - ret? Wie plötz - lich fällt, Was Alt und Jung und Reich und Arm ge - eh - ret! Was ist doch al - les, was man all- hier findt? Ein lei - chter Wind!

2 Was jetzund blüht,
Kann noch vor Abend ganz zutreten werden.
Der sich hier müht
Um flüchtig Geld, muß ohne Geld zur Erden,
Er sammlet fleißig, doch für ander, ein
Und stirbt allein.

3 Das kleine Tier,
Das Seiden spinnt, verstrickt sich in sein Spinnen,
So müssen wir
Durch unsern Fleiß oft unsern Tod gewinnen,
Viel hat Verstand, und was uns weise macht,
Ins Grab gebracht.

4 Der Tulipan
Wird, weil er glänzt, von Jungfern abgeschnitten;
Schau Menschen an!
Sie haben Schmach, um daß sie schön, erlitten,
Und, wenn sie nicht entsetzt ein schneller Tod,
Ach! Angst und Not!

5 Bist du bekannt,
So kann dir jeder deine Fehl aufrücken:
Wofern dein Stand
Verborgen liegt, so wird dich jeder drücken.
Wer reich ist, wird beneidet und verlacht,
Wer arm, der schmacht.

6 Wie ohne Ruh
Ein Schifflein wird bald her, bald hin geschmissen,
So setzt uns zu
Der Sorgen Sturm, wir werden hingerissen
Auf deines Lebens schmerzenvollen See,
Da eitel Weh!

7 Wie selig ist,
Wer schadenfrei kann an den Port einfahren!
Wer ihm erkiest
Den rechten Lauf der gottergebnen Scharen,
Der kann, ob Wellen Bergen gleich aufstehn,
Nicht untergehn.

2 Mein Seufzen, meine Bitt,
Erweichte sein Gemüt,
Daß er, der Brunn der Güt,
Vom Himmel auf mein Elend sahe,
Es sahe meinen Schmerz
Sein ewigtreues Herz,
Er zog mich aus der Wehmut Stricken,
Ja wenn ich wollt in Angst ersticken,
War er mit seinem Beistand nahe.

3 Herr, der du mich erhört,
Wenn dich mein Geist geehrt,
Wie daß mich jetzt versehrt
Der Natter Zungen tolles Zischen?
Soll mich denn jede Stund
Der Falschen Lastermund,
Das lügenreiche Maul verletzen?
Mein Gott! wenn willst du mich ergetzen,
Und diese Tränen mir abwischen?

4 Mag was mit dieser Pein
Wohl zu vergleichen sein?
Sie rennt durch Mark und Bein,
Als wenn ein Pfeil vom Bogen fähret,
Wie wenn die lichte Macht
Der Donnerflamm erkracht,
Und die Wacholdersträuch anzündet,
Daß eilend Ast und Laub verschwindet,
Und Strump und Wurzel ganz verzehret.

5 Ach! soll ich dieses Land,
In das mich deine Hand
Zum Schmerzen hat verbannt,
Mein Heiland länger noch bewohnen!
O führe mich von hier:
Herr, soll ich für und für
Bei Mesech und bei Kedar sitzen!
Was kann dir doch mein Elend nützen?
Ach Herr, komm, und fang an zu schauen.

6 Ich habe meine Zeit
In fremder Dienstbarkeit,
In Wehmut, Ach und Leid,
Bis auf den Augenblick verschwendet!
Ich sehne mich nach Ruh,
Sie richten Hader zu,
Komm führe mich, wo ich dies Leben
Nur kann zu deinem Dienst hingeben,
Bis meine Pilgerschaft vollendet.

Rauch und As - che wer-den. Kein Fels, kein Erz kann stehn. Dies,

was uns kann er - get-zen, Was wir für e - wig schät-zen, Wird

als ein lei - chter Traum ver-gehn.

2    Was sind doch alle Sachen,
Die uns ein Herze machen,
Als schlechte Nichtigkeit?
Was ist des Menschen Leben,
Der immer um muß schweben,
Als eine Phantasie der Zeit?

3    Der Ruhm, nach dem wir trachten,
Den wir unsterblich achten,
Ist nur ein falscher Wahn;
Sobald der Geist gewichen
Und dieser Mund erblichen,
Fragt keiner, was man hier getan.

4    Es hilft kein weises Wissen,
Wir werden hingerissen
Ohn einen Unterschied.
Was nützt der Schlösser Menge?
Dem hie die Welt zu enge,
Dem wird ein enges Grab zu weit.

5    Dies alles wird zerrinnen,
Was Müh und Fleiß gewinnen
Und saurer Schweiß erwirbt;
Was Menschen hier besitzen,
Kann vor dem Tod nicht nützen:
Dies alles stirbt uns, wenn man stirbt.

6    Ist eine Lust, ein Scherzen,
Das nicht ein heimlich Schmerzen
Mit Herzensangst vergällt?
Was ist's, womit wir prangen?
Wo wirst du Ehr erlangen,
Die nicht in Hohn und Schmach verfällt?

7    Was pocht man auf die Throne,
Da keine Macht noch Krone
Kann unvergänglich sein?
Es mag vom Totenreihen
Kein Szepter dich befreien,
Kein Purpur, Geld noch edler Stein.

8    Wie eine Rose blühet,
Wenn man die Sonne siehet
Begrüßen diese Welt,
Die eh der Tag sich neiget,
Eh sich der Abend zeiget,
Verwelkt und unversehns abfällt.

9    So wachsen wir auf Erden
Und hoffen, groß zu werden
Und schmerz- und sorgenfrei;
Doch eh wir zugenommen
Und recht zur Blüte kommen,
Bricht uns des Todes Sturm entzwei.

10    Wir rechnen Jahr auf Jahre,
Indessen wird die Bahre
Uns vor die Tür gebracht;
Drauf müssen wir von hinnen
Und, eh wir uns besinnen,
Der Erden sagen Gute Nacht.

dem dich grim - mig Schmer - zen    Und  har - te

Not    und Angst, die Pest der Her - zen,    Bis -

-her   ver - strickt;   Wir wol - len  sor - gen-frei

Und  kum - mer - los   des Höch - sten Güt  er -

-he - ben,  Der Sie - chen heilt  und Leich-en hei-ßet le - ben.

2    Wo find ich Wort'? Ach, Gott, wo fang ich an
Zu zählen, was mir deine Treu will gönnen,
Was kein Verstand je hat begreifen können?
Wie sprech ich aus, was niemand zählen kann?
Kein Mensch versteht die Wunder deiner Werke,
Den weisen Rat, der großen Arme Stärke.

3    Wer wird denn, Herr, die ewigfeste Treu
Ausstreichen recht? Der klugen Geister Scharen,
Die um dich her voll heißer Andacht fahren,
Sind hier zu schlecht. Die Gunst wird stündlich neu,
Durch die du dir den Kreis der Welt verbunden,
Der auf dein Wort sich in den Stand gefunden.

4    Die Liebe wächst, durch die du mich gemacht,
Da ich nicht war, durch die du mich erkoren,
Eh als ich ward, die, als ich war verloren
Durch Adams Schuld, mich dir hat wiederbracht,
Die mich so wert, da ich nichts wert, geschätzet,
Daß sie dein Kind für mich in Tod versetzet.

5    Aus wie viel Weh, aus wie viel herbem Leid
Hast du bisher mich wunderlich geführet?
Wie oft hat mich der blasse Tod berühret,
Wie oft fiel ich in Grund der Traurigkeit?
Wie oft hat mich der rauhe Schmerz gefangen,
Wie oft bin ich in Elend schier vergangen?

6    Ich bin durch Flamm und durch der Feinde Schwert,
Durch schweren Raub, durch schnelle Pestilenzen,
Durch was noch jetzt so brennt in unsern Grenzen,
Ich bin durch Sturm, der Schiff und Gut verzehrt,
Durch hohen Neid, durch grimme Schlangenzungen,
Durch List gerückt. Doch, Herr, mir ist's gelungen.

7    Weil du mir stets geboten deine Hand,
Hab ich gar oft mit Schrecken sehn vergehn
Die mir und dir, Herr, wollten widerstehn,
Du hast mein Ach und ihren Trotz gewandt.
Drum will ich, weil ich werd ein' Ader rühren,
Dein wertes Lob in meinem Munde führen.

8    Du hast mir mehr, als jemals ich begehrt,
O guter Gott, o milder Herr, gegeben:
Oft, eh ich noch die Hände wollt erheben,
War diesem Geist sein Wünschen schon gewährt:
Drum will ich, weil ich werd ein' Ader rühren,
Dein wertes Lob in meinem Munde führen.

9    Herr, fahre fort, zieh deine milde Hand
Nicht von mir ab, laß alle Menschen schauen
An mir, wie gut es sei, auf dich vertrauen,
Wenn schon sich Rat und Hilf und Trost verwandt:
So will ich, weil ich werd ein' Ader rühren,
Dein wertes Lob in meinem Munde führen.

I Was frag ich nach der Welt! Sie wird in Flam - men stehn. Was acht ich rei - che Pracht! Der Tod reißt al - les hin. Was hilft die Wis - sen-schaft, Der mehr denn fal - sche Dunst? Der Lie - be Zau - ber-werk ist tol - le Phan - ta - sie. Die Wol - lust ist für - wahr nichts als ein schnell - er Traum, Die Schön-heit ist wie Schnee; dies Le - ben ist der Tod.

2 Dies alles stinkt mich an, drum wünsch ich mir den Tod,
Weil nichts, wie schön und stark, wie reich es sei, kann stehn.
Oft, eh man leben will, ist schon das Leben hin.
Wer Schätz' und Reichtum sucht, was sucht er mehr als Dunst?
Wenn dem der Ehrenrauch entsteckt die Phantasie,
So träumt ihm, wenn er wacht, er wacht und sorgt im Traum.

3 Auf, meine Seel, auf, auf, entwach aus deinem Traum!
Verwirf, was irdisch ist, und trotze Not und Tod!
Was wird dir, wenn du wirst vor jenem Throne stehn,
Die Welt behilflich sein? Wo denken wir doch hin?
Was blendet den Verstand? Soll dieser leichte Dunst
Bezaubern mein Gemüt mit solcher Phantasie?

4 Bisher, und weiter nicht! Verfluchte Phantasie!
Nichtswertes Gaukelwerk, verblendungsvoller Traum!
Du schmerzenreiche Lust! Du folterharter Tod!
Ade, ich will nunmehr auf freien Füßen stehn
Und treten, was mich trat! Ich eile schon dahin,
Wo nichts als Wahrheit ist, kein bald verschwindend Dunst.

5 Treib, ewig helles Licht, den dicken Nebeldunst,
Die blinde Lust der Welt, die tolle Phantasie,
Die flüchtige Begierd und dieser Güter Traum
Hinweg und lehre mich recht sterben vor dem Tod!
Laß mich die Eitelkeit der Erden recht verstehn,
Entbinde mein Gemüt und nimm die Ketten hin!

6 Nimm, was mich und die Welt verkuppelt! Nimm doch hin
Der Sünden schwere Last! Laß ferner keinen Dunst
Verhüllen mein Gemüt, und alle Phantasie
Der eitel-leeren Welt sei vor mir als ein Traum,
Von dem ich nun erwacht! Und laß nach diesem Tod
Wenn hin Dunst, Phantasie, Traum, Tod, mich ewig stehn!

dies gesch-mink-ten Glück-es fal-sche Pracht, Und was be-

-tör-te Sin-nen mag er-get-zen, Mit sorg-und kum-mer-

-frei-em Mut ver-lacht, Dem kein Ver-za-gen das

Herz zu-bricht: Den kein Weh-kla-gen, Kein scheel Ge-sicht Noch Neid an-stricht!

2    Er tritt, was alles tritt, mit steifen Füßen,
Herrscht über sich und pocht der Menschen Not,
Er trotzt, was Fleisch und Jahre leiden müssen,
Er zwingt die Pest der großen Welt, den Tod.
Kann in sich finden,
Was jener sucht,
Der gleich den Blinden
In schneller Flucht
Irrt ohne Frucht.

3    Er hört mit Lust, wenn mancher rühmt und lüget,
Und höhnt den Rauch der stolzen Eitelkeit,
Er schaut, wenn mich ein falscher Freund betrüget,
Sich um nach Treu der hochbegreisten Zeit.
Er liebt nicht Liebe,
Die Wind und Dunst
Und Seelenhiebe
Gibt für die Gunst
Der keuschen Brunst.

4    Er schmückt sein ganz mit Ehr geziert Gemüte
Mit nicht gemeinem Glanz der Weisheit aus;
Er lernt, warum die stolze Welle wüte,
Er kennt die Sternen selbst in ihrem Haus.
Was in den Lüften,
Was ob uns schwebt,
Was aus den Klüften
Der Gruft erhebt
Und ewig lebt.

5    Ihm steht, was Welt und Himmel zuschließt, offen,
Er denen nur, die sein Verstand erwählt,
Von denen gleiche Seel und Gunst zu hoffen
Und Treu, die Freund erkiest und selten zählt:
Mit diesen teilet
Er Lust und Leid,
Er übereilet
Was nah und weit,
Pocht Tod und Zeit.

6    Ach! könnt ich, was ich jetzund rühm, erlangen!
Ach, mein Verhängnis, was hält mich zurück?
Wenn wird mich doch die süße Ruh umfangen,
Die schöne Lust, das allerhöchste Glück?
Mich würd ergetzen
Ein lustig Feld
Vor reichsten Schätzen,
Der Fürsten Zelt,
Ja Ehr und Welt.

I Schöp-fer, des - sen Wun - der-gü - te Mich, da ich nicht war, ge-macht,
Des - sen e - wig-treu Ge - mü - te Mich ans Licht der Welt ge-bracht:

Der du mein er-neu - tes Le - ben Mir die Nacht willst wie - der-ge - ben.

2   Vor dir beug ich Knie und Herze,
Vor dich stellt sich Seel und Geist,
Die nach überhäuftem Schmerze
Doch dein Allmacht Leben heißt,
Die längst Not und Tod verschlungen,
Wenn du mir nicht beigesprungen.

3   Dem ich nimmermehr kann danken,
Weil dein Arm mich mehr erhöht
Als in diesen Lebens-Schranken
Der bestürzte Sinn versteht,
Herr, daß ich noch hier mag bleiben,
Ist dir einig zuzuschreiben.

4   Viel! daß nicht verstellte Glieder
Die geschickte Seel beschwert,
Mehr, daß mich, was dir zuwider,
Nicht mit falschem Tand verkehrt,
Mehr, daß ich kaum hergeboren
Schon zu deinem Kind erkoren.

5   Du hast meine Sündenflecken
Durch das Taufbad abgefegt,
Daß mich Höll und Feind nicht schrecken,
Hast du rings um mich gelegt
Tausend Geister, die mich leiten,
Daß mein Fuß nicht fehl kann schreiten.

6   Du hast mir bisher gegeben
Mehr als je mein Herz begehrt,
Du hast Mittel wohl zu leben,
Wenn kein Mittel war, beschert,
Du wirst auf mein sehnlich Klagen
Mir auch keinen Trost abschlagen.

7   Unerschöpfte Macht, erscheine,
Und vollzieh, was du beginnt,
Daß ich dich, und sonst nichts, meine,
Eh des Lebens Zeit zerrinnt,
Daß ich nach nichts, als dir, frage
Bis ans Ende meiner Tage.

8   Halleluja! Tod entweiche!
Ich poch aller Grüfte Recht,
Gott will nicht, daß ich erbleiche,
Gott heißt leben seinen Knecht,
Daß er Gottes Wundersachen
Allen möge kündig machen.

I Sü - ßes Kind, der Vä - ter Hoff - en, Kind der Men - schen Lö - se-geld!
Steht der Him - mel nun-mehr off - en, Lie - fert Gott dich jetzt der Welt?

Hei - land, wirst du nun ge - bor - en, Zu er - ret - ten was ver-lor - en?

2    Eh die Welt die Zeit gekennet,
Gott ihm ewig gleich gebar
Einen Sohn, das Wort genennet,
Das im Anfang war, und wahr;
Gott, das Wort, kommt auf die Erden,
Wunder! Gott soll Fleisch hier werden!

3    Heiligkeit der höchsten Güte!
Ach! verläßt du deinen Thron?
Wie entsetzt sich mein Gemüte!
Wird Gott eines Menschen Sohn?
Den nichts, was er schuf, kann schließen,
Kann die zarte Jungfer küssen.

4    Ach, er kommt, er wird geboren,
Weil der bleiche Monden wacht,
Vor dem Licht sein Licht verloren,
Kommt verhüllt mit schwarzer Nacht,
Den viel tausend Jahr begehret,
Wird, da man's nicht meint, bescheret.

5    Doch er wird, den alle kennen,
Nicht von seinem Volk erkannt.
Der die Welt sein Haus kann nennen,
Wird in einen Stall verbannt,
Der der Erden Grund beweget,
Wird auf dürres Heu geleget.

6    Dem der Donner zu Gebote,
Dem der Blitz zu Dienste steht,
Der an Macht dem höchsten Gotte
Als auch gleich im Wesen geht,
Der, was ist, und ward, gebauet,
Wird hier als ein Kind geschauet.

7    Kann der Schöpfer ein Geschöpfe,
Kann die Jungfrau Mutter sein?
Tritt dies Kind der Drachen Köpfe
Und des Satans Scheitel ein?
Wird die Weisheit selbst zum Kinde?
Trägt die Unschuld meine Sünde?

8  Irr ich? Nein, ich schau den Himmel
Selbst mit Freuden schwanger gehn,
Und mit jauchzendem Getümmel
Tausend Engel um mich stehn!
Engel, die zu Ehren singen
Dem, der uns will Frieden bringen.

9  Alles frohlockt, alles lachet!
Nur mein hochbetrübtes Herz,
Das im Jammerfeuer krachet,
Das der martervolle Schmerz
Mit stets neuen Geißeln plaget,
Schmacht bei dieser Freud und zaget.

10  Augen, die ihr alles sehet,
Seht, was meine Seele schätzt,
Schaut, wie mich der Satan schmähet,
Schaut, wie mich die Welt verletzt,
Schaut, wie mich die Nacht erschrecket
Und mit Traurigkeit verdecket!

11  Arm, verlassen und alleine
Fall ich vor dir auf die Knie!
Und wen wunderts, daß ich weine?
Ist dies Leben nicht voll Müh?
Könnt ich wohl die Tränen zwingen,
Wenn du selbst sie mußt vordringen?

12  Wenn man Wollust traurig schauet
Und die Freude klagen hört,
Wenn vor dem der Erden grauet,
Der sich selbst der Welt verehrt,
Könnte man im Tal der Zähren
Sich denn herber Angst erwehren?

13  Doch dein Weinen bringt zuwegen,
Was allein ich wünschen soll,
Daß sich meine Schmerzen legen,
Daß mir in und durch dich wohl,
Daß ich, frei von Leid und Reuen,
Mich mit dir werd ewig freuen.

2    Wie uns die Jahr entfallen,
Weil wir auf Erden wallen,
Wie sich das Ziel abkürzt:
So wird mit ihm verloren,
Was in der Zeit geboren,
Die alles fällt und stürzt.

3   Indem ein Jahr vergangen,
Hat eines angefangen,
Den Anfang führt das End.
Vor stieg die Sonne nieder,
Jetzt kommt ihr Wagen wieder,
Der schon was höher rennt.

4   So, ob wir hier veralten,
Ob Händ' und Herz erkalten,
Gehn wir doch gar nicht ein;
So viel wir abgenommen,
So nahe sind wir kommen
Der Wollust oder Pein.

5   Ach! Menschen, diese Jahre,
Die führen nach der Bahre
Und nach der Bahr zur Kron:
Sie führen zu dem Throne,
Dem ewig hohen Lohne,
Wo nicht zu stetem Hohn.

6   Unendlich, ewig Wesen,
Durch dessen Tod genesen,
Was Zeit und Jahre zählt!
Ach, laß unendlich leben
Die, der du dich gegeben
Und ewig hast erwählt!

7   Soll sie die Zeit bewähren,
So laß sie nicht beschweren
Mit dem, was zeitlich ist;
Gib ewige Gedanken
Der, die in diesen Schranken
Zur Ewigkeit erkiest!

8   Daß, wenn sie abgeleget,
Was sie als sterblich träget,
Der rauhen Jahre Last,
Sich zu dir mög erheben,
Der du, ein Mensch, im Leben
Jahr' auch gezählet hast.

XI. *Unschuld ist der sichre Schutz*
*Wider der Verleumdung Trutz*

Mit den Lü - gen auf dich krat- zen, Hü - te dich nur vor der Tat,

Denn der— Lü - gen wird wohl Rat.

2    Wenn der höchst vergällten Herzen
    Tödliches Verleumdungsgift
    Dich und deine Seele trifft,
    O so mußt du dies verschmerzen!
    Hüte dich nur vor der Tat,
    Denn der Lügen wird wohl Rat.

3    Laß dich dieses nur nicht kränken,
    Würde doch das Licht der Welt
    Von den Hunden angebellt,
    Dieses mußt du wohl bedenken.
    Hüte dich nur vor der Tat,
    Denn der Lügen wird wohl Rat.

4    Wird der Himmel gleich umzogen
    Mit dem trüben Wolkenflor,
    So bricht doch die Sonne vor,
    Also wirst du gleich belogen.
    So vermeide nur die Tat,
    Denn der Lügen ist wohl Rat.

5    Deine Sonn wird Platz gewinnen,
    Deine Unschuld wird bestehn,
    Und die Lügen wird zergehn,
    Die die Feinde dir anspinnen.
    Hüte dich nur vor der Tat,
    Denn der Lügen ist wohl Rat.

6    Sie bestehen doch nur Schanden,
Weil ihr herbes Lügengift
Sie und ihren Schädel trifft,
Binden sich mit eignen Banden.
Aber du, fleuch böse Tat,
Sie ist wohl der Lügen Rat.

7    Du wirst deine Freude sehen,
Wenn der Feind zurückeweicht,
Und sein Pfeil dich nicht erreicht,
Laß ihn Netz und Garne drehen.
Meide du nur böse Tat,
So wird wohl der Lügen Rat.

8    Unschuld wird allein bestehen,
Unschuld ist der beste Schatz,
Sie behält dennoch den Platz,
Sie wird nimmermehr vergehen.
Wenn du fleuchst die böse Tat,
So schafft sie der Lügen Rat.

Welt A - de! Ich has - se dich. In den himm - li - schen Ge - mä - chern

Will ich, trotz der groß - ten Pein, Bei dem Her - ren Je - su sein.

2 Welt, ade! Ich habe Lust
Bald dir gute Nacht zu geben
Und an meines Jesu Brust
In gewünschter Ruh zu leben.
Dort will ich ohn alle Pein
Bei dem Herren Jesu sein.

3 Welt, ade! Bei dir ist Not,
Kummer, Schmerzen, Angst und Jammer,
Komm, o höchst gewünschter Tod,
Führ mich in die Freudenkammer,
Wo ich kann ohn alle Pein
Bei dem Herren Jesu sein.

4 Welt, ade! Du Thränental!
Sei gegrüßt, o Haus der Freuden,
Welt, ade! Du Jammersaal,
Dort will ich in Freuden weiden
Und verklärt in vollem Schein
Bei dem Herren Jesu sein.

5 Welt, ade! Ich suche Ruh,
Die ich muß bei dir vermissen,
Himmel, meine Lust, Glück zu!
Bei dir will ich Ruh genießen.
Dort werd ich, o Jesu, dein,
Und du ewig meine sein.

## 27

Ihr schö - nen Au - gen! Ihr hel - ler Glanz! Wer

wird euch tau - gen, ihr— blen - det ganz!

Ihr hel - len Ster - - ne— scheint ge - gen

mir, Als wie von fer - ne, des— Him - mels Zier.

## 28

Nir - gend hin als auf den Mund, da sinkts in— dem Her - zens-

From: A. Schering, *Geschichte der Musik in Beispielen*, Breitkopf and Härtel.

## 29

From: *Denkmäler deutscher Tonkunst*, Erste Folge, xlvi/xlvii, Breitkopf and Härtel.

Kommt, ihr Stun - den, ihr Stun - den, macht mich

frei,                    Kommt, ihr Stun - den, ihr

Stun - den, macht mich frei    Von    des ___

Le - bens, von des Le - bens Ty - ran - nei, von des

Le - - - - - - - - bens, Ty - ran-

-nei. Glaubt, ich weiß micht nicht nicht zu

fas - sen, mei-ne Qual ist all - zu groß, mei - ne Qual ist

all - zu_ groß, mei - ne Qual, mei - ne Qual ist all - zu

groß; Ich steh al - ler Hoff - nung los Ganz ver - las -

- sen.

Kommt, ihr Stun - den, ihr

Stun - den macht mich frei, Kommt, ihr

Stun - den, ihr Stun - den macht mich frei Von des Le - bens, von des

Le - bens Ty - ran - nei, von des Le -

- bens Ty - ran - nei.

# 31

Das zit - tern - de Glän - zen der spie - len - den Wel - len Ver sil - bert das U - fer, be -

- per - let den Strand, das zit - tern - de_ Glän - zen der spie - len - den Wel -

- - - - len ver - sil - bert das U - fer, ver - sil - bert das U - fer, be - per -

- - - - let den Strand, das

zit - tern - de_ Glän - zen der spie - len - den Wel - len ver - sil - bert das U - fer, be - per - let den Strand, das

zit - tern - de Glän - zen der spie - len - den Wel - len ver - sil - bert das U - fer, be - per -

- - - - let - den Strand, das

From: Handel, *Neun Deutsche Arien*, ed. H. Roth, Breitkopf and Härtel.

# 32

sanf - te Quel - le ru - hi - ger___

___ Ge - las - sen - heit, ru - hi - ger

Ge - las - sen - heit!

Selbst die See-le, selbst die See-le wird er-freut,

wenn ich_ mir nach die-ser_ Zeit

ar-beit-sa-mer Ei-tel-keit je-ne

Ruh, je-ne Ruh vor Au-gen stel-le, die uns_

From: Handel, *Neun Deutsche Arien*, ed. H. Roth, Breitkopf and Härtel.

## 33

Lie-ben ist ein Werk der Göt - ter: Drum ver-denkt es
Ihr ver-ruch-ten Lie-bes-spöt - ter, Daß mein Herz drauf

mir doch nicht, Weil ich le-be, will_ ich lie-ben,
ab - ge - richt.

Und_ mich in dem an - ge-neh-men We-sen ü - ben

From: *Denkmäler deutscher Tonkunst,* Erste Folge, xxxv/xxxvi, Breitkopf and Härtel.

## 34

*Unschuldig*

An die - ser schat - ten - rei - chen Lin - de,_ wo
In de - ren grün - lich brau - ne Rin - de_ ich

schon mein Va - ter schlief und sang, In die - sem Klee,_ an
neu - lich Phyl-lis Na - men schlang,

die - sem Ba - che, der mei - ne Scha - fe

tränt und kühlt, hier lieg ich, spie - le, sin - ge,

la - che und schla - fe wenn ich gnug ge - spielt.

From: *Denkmäler deutscher Tonkunst,* Erste Folge, lvii, Breitkopf and Härtel.

## 35

*Augenehm*

Uns lockt die Mor-gen - rö - te in Busch und Wald, wo

schon des Schäf-ers Flö - te ins Land er - schallt. Die

Ler - che steigt und schwir - ret, von Lust er - regt; die

Tau - be lacht und gir - ret, die Wach - tel schlägt.

From: *Denkmäler deutscher Tonkunst,* Erste Folge, lvii, Breitkopf and Härtel.

# APPENDIX B

## Notes on Recordings

THIS is not a comprehensive list. Musical experts will in any case have all the information they need. These notes take account rather of those who may appreciate guidance of quite a simple kind. Also, no reference is made to records that have been withdrawn or for any reason are difficult to obtain. Most of those mentioned are in the *Archive* series of the Deutsche Grammophon Gesellschaft, distinguished by the consistent endeavour to perform older works in as historically correct a way as possible. Unless otherwise stated, references are to this series.

Problems concerning figural music, touched on in the Introduction, can be usefully followed up with the help of APM 14023 and APM 14131, performances respectively of Schütz's *Musicalische Exequien* and of motets from his *Geistliche Chormusik*. Among the latter, incidentally, is a setting of *Die mit Tränen säen*, providing a valuable point of comparison with Schein's setting of the same text (referred to in Chapter IV). Regarding Chapter I, EPA 35007 enables one to hear three of Senfl's polyphonic songs, and in conjunction with instruments of the period (viols, recorders, and lute). AP 13030 contains a selection of pieces from the *Glogauer Liederbuch*, both vocal and instrumental, and here too the authentic sound of the correct instruments will be a valuable experience for those unaccustomed to this earlier music. Some of Lasso's German songs are available on APM 14055 together with examples of his other secular music. The magnificent recording of Lasso's *Seven Penitential Psalms* on APM 14129/30 will be useful for wider reference and for the contrast of a more sombre style. In connexion with Chapter II the *balletti* of Gastoldi on APM 14042 have incidental interest. The representative selection of Hassler's *Neüe teütsche gesang* (including items from the *Lustgarten*, and with pieces by Lechner on the other side) on APM 14010 is indispensable for anyone wishing to study further the music of Hassler, discussed in Chapter III, and there is a Latin motet of Hassler on EPA 37179. Madrigals of Marenzio (APM 14045), Gesualdo (APM 14132), and Monteverdi (APM 14020) have a bearing on several aspects of the text, particularly in the case of Chapter IV, and relevant for the same chapter are the examples of fantasia music on APM 14056 (devoted to the work of Orlando Gibbons). Some background considerations in Chapter V call for mention of the songs of Morley and Dowland on EPA 37097 and EPA 37010. For Chapter VII there is the splendid recording on APM 14035 of a wide selection of Krieger's songs; the continuo realizations are models of their kind, and the adoption of a lower pitch is an interesting period touch. It is in this chapter that reference is made to Bach's *Goldberg Variations*, played on the harpsichord by Ralph Kirkpatrick on APM 14135. There is little, unfortunately, to be said in this connexion about Chapters VIII, IX, and X—it would, by the way, fill an important gap if Briegel's songs were put on disc. The *History of Music in Sound* offers a recording of Erlebach's

*Meine Seufzer, meine Klagen* (HMS 6), and a *Musica Mundi* (Schwann edition) record (MMD 2) contains two of his songs. The superb performance and recording of Handel's *Neun Deutsche Arien* on APM 14031, the subject of Chapter XII, has the merit, apart from the excellence of the singing, of using baroque-type instruments in the obligati, with impressive and sometimes unexpected effect. An interesting and in some respects amusing epilogue to this book is provided by APM 14066, a recording of pieces from the *Ohren-Vergnügendes und Gemüths-ergötzendes Tafelconfect* of Rathgeber and Seyfert, constituting a sort of short anthology of songs popular in the early eighteenth century.

# BIBLIOGRAPHY

A MORE or less comprehensive list of relevant works in two different fields would be unjustifiably long, and so I have concentrated in this bibliography mainly on those that I have found of exceptional value for general aspects or of special interest concerning particular problems.

ABER, A., *Handbuch der Musikliteratur in systematisch-chronologischer Anordnung*, Leipzig, 1922.

ABERT, Anna Amalie, *Die stilistischen Voraussetzungen der 'Cantiones sacrae' von Heinrich Schütz*, Wolfenbüttel and Berlin, 1935.

ABERT, H., 'Wort und Ton in der Musik des 18. Jahrhunderts', *Gesammelte Schriften und Vorträge*, ed. F. Blume, Halle, 1929.

—— 'Entstehung und Wurzeln des begleiteten deutschen Sololiedes', ibid.

ALBIN, F., *Johann Klaj*, Marburg, 1908.

AUDEN, W. H., KALLMANN, C., and GREENBERG, N., *An Elizabethan Song Book*, London, 1957.

BALET, L., *Die Verbürgerlichung der deutschen Kunst, Literatur und Musik im 18. Jahrhundert*, Strassburg, 1936.

BECKER-GLAUCH, Irmgard, *Die Bedeutung der Musik für die Dresdner Hoffeste*, Cassel and Basel, 1951.

BERGER, K., 'Die Dichtung im Zusammenhang der Künste', *Deutsche Vierteljahrschrift für Literaturwissenschaft und Geistesgeschichte*, xxi, 1943.

BESSELER, H., *Die Musik des Mittelalters und der Renaissance*, Potsdam, 1931.

BLACKALL, E. A., *The Emergence of German as a Literary Language*, Cambridge, 1959.

BLUME, F. (ed.), *Die Musik in Geschichte und Gegenwart*, Cassel and Basel, 1949 seqq.

—— *Das monodische Prinzip in der protestantischen Kirchenmusik*, Leipzig, 1925.

BOCKMANN, P., *Formgeschichte der deutschen Dichtung*, Hamburg, 1949.

BOETTICHER, W., *Orlando di Lasso und seine Zeit*, Cassel and Basel, 1958.

—— *Von Palestrina zu Bach*, Stuttgart, 1959.

BORCHERDT, H. H., *Augustus Buchner und seine Bedeutung für die deutsche Literatur des 17. Jahrhunderts*, Munich, 1919.

BRAUER, W., 'Jakob Regnart, J. H. Schein und die Anfänge der deutschen Barocklyrik', *Deutsche Vierteljahrschrift für Literaturwissenschaft und Geistesgeschichte*, xvii, 1939.

BRÜGGEMANN, F., *Die bürgerliche Gemeinschaftskultur der vierziger Jahre (Deutsche Literatur in Entwicklungsreihen, Reihe Aufklärung: 5)*, Leipzig, 1933.

BÜCKEN, E., *Das deutsche Lied*, Hamburg, 1939.

—— *Die Musik des Rokokos und der Klassik*, Potsdam, 1927.

—— *Geist und Form im musikalischen Kunstwerk*, Potsdam, 1929.

BUKOFZER, M. F., *Music in the Baroque Era*, New York, 1947.

BULLIVANT, R., 'Word-Painting and Chromaticism in the Music of J. S. Bach', *Music Review*, Aug.–Nov. 1959.

BUSCH, G., *C. P. E. Bach und seine Lieder*, Regensburg, 1957.

CHRYSANDER, F., *G. F. Händel*, Leipzig, 1858–67.

DAMMANN, R., 'Die Musiklehre des Andreas Werckmeister', *Archiv für Musikwissenschaft*, xi, 1954.

DART, T., *The Interpretation of Music*, London, 1954.

EGGEBRECHT, H. H., 'Das Ausdrucksprinzip im musikalischen Sturm und Drang', *Deutsche Vierteljahrschrift für Literaturwissenschaft und Geistesgeschichte*, xxix, 1955.

—— 'Barock als musikgeschichtliche Epoche', *Aus der Welt des Barock* (by various hands), Stuttgart, 1957.

—— 'Über Bachs geschichtlichen Ort', *Deutsche Vierteljahrschrift für Literaturwissenschaft und Geistesgeschichte*, xxxi, 1957.

EINSTEIN, A., 'Ein unbekannter Druck aus der Frühzeit der deutschen Monodie', *Sammelbände der Internationalen Musikgesellschaft*, xiii, 1911–12.

EITNER, R., *Bibliographie der Musiksammelwerke*, Berlin, 1877.

—— *Das deutsche Lied des 15. und 16. Jahrhunderts*, Berlin, 1876–80.

—— edition of *Seelewig*, *Monatshefte für Musikgeschichte*, xiii, 1881.

—— 'Das ältere deutsche mehrstimmige Lied und seine Meister', *Monatshefte für Musikgeschichte*, xxv–xxvi, 1893/4.

ELIOT, T. S., *The Music of Poetry*, Glasgow, 1942.

EVANS, M., *English Poetry in the Sixteenth Century*, London, 1955.

FABER DU FAUR, C. von, 'Johann Khuen', *Publications of the Modern Language Association of America*, lxiv, 1949.

FELLOWES, E. H., *English Madrigal Composers*, Oxford, 1921.

—— *The English Madrigal*, London, 1935.

FISCHER, A., *Das deutsche evangelische Kirchenlied des 17. Jahrhunderts*, Gütersloh, 1902.

FISCHER, K., *Gabriel Voigtländer, ein Dichter und Musiker des 17. Jahrhunderts* (Diss.), Berlin, 1910.

FISCHER, L. F., 'Fremde Melodien in Heinrich Alberts Arien', *Vierteljahrschrift für Musikwissenschaft*, ii, 1886.

FLEMMING, W., *Der Wandel des deutschen Naturgefühls vom 15. zum 18. Jahrhundert*, Halle, 1931.

—— *Die Oper* (*Deutsche Literatur in Entwicklungsreihen, Reihe Barock: 5*), Leipzig, 1933.

—— *Oratorium, Festspiel* (ibid. 6), Leipzig, 1933.

—— *Deutsche Kultur im Zeitalter des Barock*, Potsdam, 1937.

—— 'Die Fuge als epochales Kompositionsprinzip des Barock', *Deutsche Vierteljahrschrift für Literaturwissenschaft und Geistesgeschichte*, xxxii, 1958.

FRIEDLÄNDER, M., *Das deutsche Lied im 18. Jahrhundert*, Stuttgart, 1902.

FÜRSTENAU, M., *Zur Geschichte der Musik und des Theaters am Hofe der Kurfürsten von Sachsen, Johann Georg II, Johann Georg III und Johann Georg IV*, Dresden, 1861.

GEERING, A., Introduction to Senfl's *Deutsche Lieder* in *Reichsdenkmale deutscher Musik*, Wolfenbüttel and Berlin, 1938.

—— 'Textierung und Besetzung in Ludwig Senfls Liedern', *Archiv für Musikwissenschaft*, ii, 1939.

GEORGIADES, T., *Musik und Sprache, Das Wesen der abendländischen Musik dargestellt an der Vertonung der Messe*, Berlin–Göttingen–Heidelberg, 1954.

GIRDLESTONE, C. M., *Jean-Philippe Rameau*, London, 1957.

GOLDSCHMIDT, H., *Die Musikästhetik des 18. Jahrhunderts*, Leipzig, 1915.

GUDEWILL, K., *Das sprachliche Urbild bei Heinrich Schütz* (Diss.), Cassel, 1936.

GURLITT, W., 'Form in der Musik als Zeitgestaltung', *Akademie der Wissenschaften und der Literatur in Mainz, Abhandlungen der Geistes- und Sozialwissenschaftlichen Klasse*, 1954.

HAAS, R., *Musik des Barocks*, Potsdam, 1928.

—— *Aufführungspraxis der Musik*, Potsdam, 1931.

HALLBAUM, F., *Der Landschaftsgarten, seine Entstehung und Einführung in Deutschland*, Munich, 1927.

HANKAMER, P., *Die Sprache, ihr Begriff und ihre Deutung im 16. und 17. Jahrhundert*, Bonn, 1927.

—— *Deutsche Gegenreformation und deutsches Barock*, Stuttgart, 1935.

HARTLAUB, G. F., 'Die Musik im Generalbaßzeitalter', *Deutsche Vierteljahrschrift für Literaturwissenschaft und Geistesgeschichte*, xvi, 1938.

HECKMANN, H., 'Der Takt in der Musiklehre des 17. Jahrhunderts', *Archiv für Musikwissenschaft*, x, 1935.

HEUSS, A., Introduction to edition of Krieger's *Arien* in *Denkmäler deutscher Tonkunst*, Leipzig, 1905.

HIRSCHMANN, C. F., *W. O. Briegel* (Diss.), Marburg, 1931.

HITZEROTH, C., *Johann Heermann*, Marburg, 1907.

HOFER, G., *Die Rudolstädter Festspiele und die Dichter in Probefahrten*, Leipzig, 1904.

HÖPFNER, E., *Reformbestrebungen auf dem Gebiete der deutschen Dichtung des 16. und 17. Jahrhunderts*, Berlin, 1886.

ING, C. M., *Elizabethan Lyrics*, London, 1951.

JUST, K. G., 'Musik und Dichtung', *Deutsche Philologie im Aufriß*, ed. W. Stammler, Berlin, 1957.

KADE, R., 'Christoph Demant, 1567–1643', *Vierteljahrschrift für Musikwissenschaft*, vi, 1890.

KATZ, E., *Die musikalischen Stilbegriffe des 17. Jahrhunderts* (Diss.), Freiburg i. Br., 1926.

KAUFFMANN, F., *Deutsche Metrik nach ihrer geschichtlichen Entwicklung*, Marburg, 1897.

KAYSER, W., *Die Klangmalerei bei Harsdörffer*, Leipzig, 1932.

KINKELDEY, O., Introduction to edition of Erlebach's *Harmonische Freude* in *Denkmäler deutscher Tonkunst*, Leipzig, 1914.

KLESSMANN, E., 'Die Deutschlandreisen John Dowlands', *Musica*, 1957.

KOCH, W., 'Das Fortleben Pindars in der deutschen Literatur', *Euphorion*, xxviii, 1927.

KORFF, H. A., *Geist der Goethezeit*, i, Leipzig, 1923.

KÖSTER, A., *Der Dichter der Geharnischten Venus*, Marburg, 1897.

KRABBE, W., *Johann Rist und das deutsche Lied* (Diss.), Berlin, 1910.

KRAPP, A., *Die ästhetischen Tendenzen Philipp Harsdörffers*, Berlin, 1903.

KRAUSE, H., *Johann Beer. Zur Musikauffassung des 17. Jahrhunderts* (Diss.) Leipzig, 1935.

KRETZSCHMAR, H., *Geschichte des neuen deutschen Liedes*, Leipzig, 1911.

—— Introduction to edition of Albert's *Arien* in *Denkmäler deutscher Tonkunst*, Leipzig, 1903.

LEICHTENTRITT, H., *Music, History and Ideas*, Harvard, 1938.

LEWIS, C. Day, *The Poetic Image*, London, 1947.

LILIENCRON, R. von, 'Die Horazischen Metren in deutschen Kompositionen des 16. Jahrhunderts', *Vierteljahrschrift für Musikwissenschaft*, iii, 1887.

LINDNER, E. D., *Geschichte des deutschen Liedes im 18. Jahrhundert*, Leipzig, 1871.

LUNDING, E., 'German Baroque Literature: A Synthetic View', *German Life and Letters*, iii, 1949.

MANHEIMER, V., *Die Lyrik des Andreas Gryphius*, Berlin, 1904.

MAX, H., *Martin Opitz als geistlicher Dichter*, Heidelberg, 1931.

MAYER, A., 'Zu Opitz's "Daphne" ', *Euphorion*, xxiv, 1918.

MELLERS, W., 'Words and Music in Elizabethan England', *The Age of Shakespeare*, ed. B. Ford (*The Pelican Guide to English Literature*, 2), Harmondsworth, 1955.

MENKE, W., *Das Vokalwerk Telemanns*, 1941.

MEYER, E. H., *Aufsätze über Musik*, Berlin, 1957.

MOSER, H. J., *Geschichte der deutschen Musik*, i, Stuttgart and Berlin, 1920.

—— 'Renaissance-Lyrik deutscher Musiker', *Deutsche Vierteljahrschrift für Literaturwissenschaft und Geistesgeschichte*, v, 1927.

—— *Paul Hofhaimer, ein Lied- und Orgelmeister des deutschen Humanismus*, Stuttgart and Berlin, 1929.

—— *Corydon, Geschichte des mehrstimmigen Generalbaßliedes und des Quodlibets im deutschen Barock*, Brunswick, 1933.

—— *Heinrich Schütz. Sein Leben und sein Werk*, Cassel, 1936.

—— *The German Solo Song and Ballad*, Cologne, 1958 (in *Anthology of Music*, ed. K. G. Fellerer).

MOSER, P., *Christian Gryphius*, Würzburg, 1936.

MÜLLER, G., *Geschichte des deutschen Liedes*, Munich, 1925.

—— *Deutsche Dichtung von der Renaissance bis zum Ausgang des Barock*, Potsdam, 1927.

MÜLLER-BLATTAU, J. F., *Das Kompositionsprinzip Heinrich Schützens in der Fassung seines Schülers Christoph Bernard*, Leipzig, 1926.

—— *Geschichte der deutschen Musik*, 4th ed., Berlin, 1944.

MÜTZELL, J., *Geistliche Lieder der evangelischen Kirche aus dem 17. und der ersten Hälfte des 18. Jahrhunderts*, Brunswick, 1858.

NETTL, P., *Das Wiener Lied im Zeitalter des Barock*, Vienna and Leipzig, 1934.

NIESSEN, W. M., *Das Liederbuch des Leipziger Studenten Clodius vom Jahre 1669* (Diss.), Leipzig, 1891.

NOACK, F., 'W. C. Briegel als Liederkomponist', *Musikforschung*, ii, 1949.

OSTHOFF, H., *Adam Krieger*, Leipzig, 1929.

—— *Die Niederländer und das deutsche Lied*, Berlin, 1938.

PATTISON, B., *Music and Poetry in the English Renaissance*, London, 1948.

PIRRO, A., *L'Esthétique de J. S. Bach*, Paris, 1907.

PLATEL, Marguerite, *Vom Volkslied zum Gesellschaftslied*, Berne and Leipzig, 1939.

PRÜFER, H., *J. H. Schein*, Leipzig, 1895.

—— *Johann Hermann Schein und das weltliche deutsche Lied des 17. Jahrhunderts*, Leipzig, 1908.

PYRITZ, H., *Paul Flemings deutsche Liebeslyrik*, Leipzig, 1932.

RADECKE, E., *Das deutsche weltliche Lied in der Lautenmusik des 16. Jahrhunderts* (Diss.), Leipzig, 1891.

REBLING, E., *Die soziologischen Grundlagen der Stilwandlung der Musik in Deutschland um die Mitte des 18. Jahrhunderts* (Diss.), Saalfeld, 1935.

REDLICH, H. F., 'Schein and the German Madrigal', *The Listener*, 14 April 1955.

REESE, G., *Music in the Renaissance*, London, 1954.

REISSMANN, A., *Das deutsche Lied in seiner historischen Entwicklung*, Cassel, 1861.

RIEBER, K. F., *Die Entwicklung der deutschen Solokantate im 17. Jahrhundert* (Diss.), Lörrach, 1932.

RIEMANN, H., *Handbuch der Musikgeschichte*, ii, 2 (*Das Generalbaßzeitalter*), 2nd ed., Leipzig, 1922.

RIETRICH, H., 'Heinrich Isaac und das Innsbruckslied', *Jahrbuch der Musikbibliothek Peters*, xix, 1917.

ROTSCHILD, F., *The Lost Tradition in Music. Rhythm and Tempo in J. S. Bach's Time*, London, 1953.

SACHS, C., 'Barockmusik', *Jahrbuch der Musikbibliothek Peters*, xxi, 1919.

—— *World History of the Dance*, New York, 1937.

—— *Rhythm and Tempo. A Study in Music History*, London, 1953.

SANDBERGER, A., Introduction to edition of Hassler's *Canzonette* and *Neüe teütsche gesang* in *Denkmäler deutscher Tonkunst*, Leipzig, 1904.

SCHÄFKE, R., 'Quantz als Ästhetiker. Eine Einführung in die Musikästhetik des galanten Stils', *Archiv für Musikwissenschaft*, vi, 1924.

SCHERING, A., *Bachs Textbehandlung*, Leipzig, 1900.

—— 'Die Musikästhetik der deutschen Aufklärung', *Zeitschrift der Internationalen Musikgesellschaft*, viii, 1907.

—— 'Takt und Sinngliederung in der Musik des 16. Jahrhunderts', *Archiv für Musikwissenschaft*, ii, 1920.

—— *Musikgeschichte Leipzigs, 1650–1723*, Leipzig, 1926.

—— *Geschichte der Musik in Beispielen*, Leipzig, 1931.

SCHMITZ, A., *Die Bildlichkeit in der wortgebundenen Musik J. S. Bachs*, Mainz, 1950.

—— 'Die Figurenlehre in den theoretischen Werken J. G. Walthers', *Archiv für Musikwissenschaft*, ix, 1952.

SCHMITZ, E., 'Zur musikalischen Bedeutung der Harsdörfferischen "Frauenzimmergesprächspiele"', *Liliencron-Festschrift*, Leipzig, 1910.

—— *Geschichte der weltlichen Solokantate*, Leipzig, 1914.

SCHREIBER, Irmtrud, *Dichtung und Musik der deutschen Opernarien 1680–1700* (Diss.), Bottrop i.W., 1934.

SCHWARZ, R., 'Hans Leo Hassler unter dem Einfluß der italienischen Madrigalisten', *Vierteljahrschrift für Musikwissenschaft*, ix, 1893.

SEIFFERT, M., 'Händels deutsche Gesänge', *Liliencron-Festschrift*, Leipzig, 1910.

SERAUKY, W., *Musikgeschichte der Stadt Halle*, Halle and Berlin, 1935–42.
SPITTA, P., 'Sperontes Singende Muse an der Pleiße', *Musikalische Aufsätze*, Berlin, 1894.
—— 'Die Anfänge madrigalischer Dichtung in Deutschland', ibid.
—— *J. S. Bach*, London, 1899.
STAMM, R. (ed.), *Kunstformen des Barockzeitalters*, Berne, 1956.
STEVENS, D. (ed.), *A History of Song*, London, 1960.
STRICH, F., 'Der lyrische Stil des 17. Jahrhunderts', *Abhandlungen zur deutschen Literaturgeschichte, Franz Muncker zum 60. Geburtstage dargebracht*, Munich, 1916.
—— 'Renaissance und Reformation', *Dichtung und Zivilisation*, Munich, 1928.
STRUNK, O. (ed.), *Source Readings in Music History*, London, 1952.
SZYROCKI, M., *Martin Opitz*, Berlin, 1956.
TAUBERT, O., *Daphne, das erste deutsche Operntext*, Torgau, 1879.
THIELEN, P. G., *Die Kultur am Hofe Herzog Albrechts von Preußen, 1628–68*, Göttingen, 1953.
THOMAS, R. Hinton, 'Fugal Principles and German Baroque Poetry', *German Life and Letters*, xiii, 1960.
TRUNZ, E., 'Die Erforschung der deutschen Barockdichtung', *Deutsche Vierteljahrschrift für Literaturwissenschaft und Geistesgeschichte*, xviii, 1940.
—— 'Weltbild und Dichtung im deutschen Barock', *Aus der Welt des Barock* (by various hands), Stuttgart, 1957.
UNGER, H. J., *Die Beziehungen zwischen Musik und Rhetorik im 16.–18. Jahrhundert*, Würzburg, 1941.
URSPRUNG, O., 'Vier Studien zur Geschichte des deutschen Liedes' (4), *Archiv für Musikwissenschaft*, vi, 1923.
VELTEN, R., *Das ältere Gesellschaftslied unter dem Einfluß der italienischen Musik*, Heidelberg, 1914.
VETTER, W., 'Wort und Weise im deutschen Kunstlied', *Zeitschrift für Musikwissenschaft*, x, 1927–8.
—— *Das frühdeutsche Lied*, 2 vols., Münster, 1928.
VIETOR, K., 'Vom Stil und Geist der deutschen Barockdichtung', *Germanisch-Romanische Monatsschrift*, xiv, 1926.
—— *Probleme der deutschen Barockliteratur*, Leipzig, 1928.
VOLKMANN, H., 'Johann Nauwachs Leben', *Zeitschrift für Musikwissenschaft*, iv, 1922.
VOSSLER, K., *Das deutsche Madrigal*, Weimar, 1898.
WALDBERG, Max Freiherr von, *Die galante Lyrik*, Strassburg, 1885.
—— *Die deutsche Renaissance-Lyrik*, Berlin, 1888.
WEISBACH, W., *Der Barock als Kunst der Gegenreformation*, Berlin, 1921.
WELLECK, A., 'Renaissance- und Barock-Synästhesie', *Deutsche Vierteljahrschrift für Literaturwissenschaft*, ix, 1931.
WELLESZ, E., 'The Beginning of Baroque Opera', *Essays on Music*, London, 1950.
WIESE, B. von (ed.), *Die deutsche Lyrik*, i, Düsseldorf, 1956.
WINTERFELD, C. von, *Der evangelische Kirchengesang*, Leipzig, 1843.
WITKOWSKI, G., *Geschichte des literarischen Lebens in Leipzig*, Leipzig and Berlin, 1909.

WOLFF, H. C., *Die Barockoper in Hamburg, 1678–1738*, Wolfenbüttel, 1957.

WOODFILL, W. L., *Musicians in English Society from Elizabeth to Charles I*, Princeton, 1953.

WOOLDRIDGE, H. E., 'The Treatment of the Words in Polyphonic Music', *The Musical Antiquary*, i, 1910.

WUSTMANN, R., *Musikgeschichte Leipzigs, bis zur Mitte des 17. Jahrhunderts*, Leipzig, 1909.

YATES, F. A., *The French Academies of the Sixteenth Century*, London, 1947.

ZAHN, J., *Die Melodien der deutschen evangelischen Kirchenlieder*, Gütersloh, 1890.

# INDEX

PRINTED IN GREAT BRITAIN
AT THE UNIVERSITY PRESS, OXFORD
BY VIVIAN RIDLER
PRINTER TO THE UNIVERSITY